What Price Civil Justice?

Brian G. M. Main
University of Edinburgh

and

Alan Peacock
David Hume Institute

with a commentary by

Bruce L. Benson
Florida State University

Published by The Institute of Economic Affairs
2000

First published in January 2000 by
The Institute of Economic Affairs
2 Lord North Street
Westminster
London SW1P 3LB

© The Institute of Economic Affairs 2000

Hobart Paper 139
All rights reserved
ISBN 0-255 36429-6

Printed in Great Britain by
Hartington Fine Arts Limited, Lancing,
West Sussex

Contents

3

4

FOREWORD

Systems of civil justice in England and Wales and in Scotland have been subjected to close scrutiny in recent years. Reforms have been introduced aimed at lowering costs and reducing delays in the dispensation of justice. But reform is not just a matter for lawyers. Economists have a distinctive contribution to make because of their concerns both for efficiency in the short run and for the factors which stimulate innovation over the long term.

In Hobart Paper, Professors Brian Main and Sir Alan Peacock – two distinguished economists with interests in legal issues – use economic principles to great effect in exploring the efficiency of the civil justice system and ways in which a more innovative regime might be introduced.

They acknowledge that many good ideas are already in circulation – fast-track procedures, judicial case management, conditional fees, contingent fees and franchising of legal aid. But, they argue, instead of trying to work out *ex ante* which ideas should be implemented and how they should be combined, there is a good case for experimentation with procedural reform. Market forces should therefore have a larger rôle in the civil justice system and more competition is required in the provision of dispute resolution services of all kinds.

Features of a reformed judicial system – more efficient, more responsive to individual needs and more innovative – would, in their view, be:

■ competitive tendering and incentives for suppliers of legal services to provide full information;

■ better information for clients about alternative ways of pursuing or defending prospective actions;

- more power for trial judges to control the passage of a case;

- a supply of judges and court fees which would respond to market signals. There could, for instance, be a 'market-led expansion of judicial capacity by allowing court fees to be determined by market forces with the proceeds ploughed back into judicial capacity'.

Professor Main and Sir Alan make a strong case that reform is required to maximize benefits to consumers of justice. Failure to accept the need for reform would, they say, leave the legal profession open to the charge that it is running the system in its own interests.

One route to reform which Main and Peacock mention is increased use of alternative dispute-resolution (ADR) procedures. The Institute therefore asked Professor Bruce Benson, the leading authority in the United States on these procedures, to expand on their possible uses in a Commentary on the Main and Peacock paper.

Professor Benson draws on his extensive writings on the subject to provide a powerful exposition of the value of ADR and to dismiss many of the common objections to it. He points out, for example, that ADR is not just a procedural option for resolution of disputes. There are procedural benefits but, in addition, ADR allows the parties a choice of jurisdictions.

ADR is also a source of precedent in customary law, according to Professor Benson. The claim that ADR does not produce external benefits (in particular, precedents) as does conventional litigation is a misunderstanding: ADR providers have incentives to make careful rulings based on recognized practices, customs and precedents and they create precedents of their own to the extent they are required.

Benson rejects the view that ADR can only work where it is backed by the threat of litigation. Where repeated dealings and reputation are important, a community of transactors will abide by contractual obligations and accept arbitration decisions.

6

Finally, he claims as a big advantage of ADR that it avoids monopolized law. Monopoly in the law, as elsewhere, has undesirable results, such as inflexibility, the persistence of bad rules and difficulty in evaluating how good or bad rules are because alternatives do not exist. Moreover, monopolized law leads to politicization and produces deadweight losses through wealth transfers and bigger losses through rent-seeking.

Civil law reform is a significant area for economic analysis: the system absorbs considerable resources and yet is not subject to the pressures to operate efficiently and to be innovative which exist in many other parts of the economy. All IEA papers express the view of their authors, not those of the Institute (which has no corporate view), its Trustees, Directors or Advisers. But anyone reading the imaginative proposals in this Hobart Paper is bound to be impressed by the need for reform, on both sides of the Atlantic, and by the abundance of ideas which the three authors have produced.

October 1999   **COLIN ROBINSON**
Editorial Director, Institute of Economic Affairs
Professor of Economics, University of Surrey

THE AUTHORS

BRIAN G. M. MAIN is Professor of Economics at the University of Edinburgh and Director of The David Hume Institute. Between 1987 and 1991 he was Professor and Chairman of the Department of Economics at the University of St Andrews. His research has been predominantly in the area of labour economics. More recently, his interests have extended to include law and economics, with a recent project involving experimental studies of negotiation in the shadow of the law. He is a Fellow of the Royal Society of Edinburgh. Recent publications include articles on top executive pay in the *Economic Journal* (1996) and on pre-trial bargaining in the *Scottish Law & Practice Quarterly* (1999).

SIR ALAN PEACOCK retired from his last full-time academic post as the first Vice-Chancellor and Professor of Economics at the University of Buckingham in 1985, the year in which he co-founded The David Hume Institute, Edinburgh, and became its first Executive Director (1985–91). He is now 'enjoyably busy' writing on the economics of public policy covering such diverse fields as public choice analysis, the economics of civil justice and, unusually, the economics of the arts. He is a Fellow of the British Academy, the Royal Society of Edinburgh and the Italian National Academy, and his long-standing connection with the IEA has been recognized by an Honorary Fellowship. His recent publications include *Public Choice Analysis in Historical Perspective* (1992) and *The Political Economy of Economic Freedom* (1997).

BRUCE L. BENSON, DeVoe Moore Distinguished Research Professor at Florida State University, received his PhD in

economics from Texas A&M University in 1978. He has published more than 100 articles in academic journals and over 30 chapters in edited volumes on the economics of law and crime, public choice, and spatial economics. His most recent books are *The Enterprise of Law: Justice without the State* (1990), *The Economic Anatomy of a Drug War: Criminal Justice in the Commons* (1994 with David W. Rasmussen), and *To Serve and Protect: Privatization and Community In Criminal Justice* (1998). In addition to being appointed as DeVoe Moore Professor in Florida State University's College of Social Sciences in 1997 and honoured with the University's 1993 Distinguished Research Professor Award, Professor Benson received *The Journal of Private Enterprise* Best Paper Award (1999), the Georgescu-Roegen Prize in Economics for the best article in the Southern Economic Journal (1989), a Ludwig von Mises prize for scholarship in 'Austrian School Economics' (1992), and an honourable mention runner up for the 1991 Free Press Association's H. L. Mencken National Book Award for *The Enterprise of Law*.

I. Introduction

The costs of justice to both the taxpayer and the litigant appear to have risen faster than GDP in recent years, and it is scarcely surprising that both Conservative and Labour Governments, concerned about public expenditure trends, have brought expenditure on the courts and on legal aid under close scrutiny. In England and Wales escalating spending on legal aid in civil actions has led to the introduction of a franchising system and a significant move towards no-win-no-fee arrangements in cases where personal injury damages are involved.[1] In Scotland, the passage of the Crime and Punishment (Scotland) Act 1997 allows for the introduction of state-employed public defenders for criminal legal aid work – widely seen as a cost-curtailing measure. In his introduction to the White Paper *Modernising Justice* (1998), the Lord Chancellor emphasizes the importance of obtaining recourse to the civil courts at a cost that is predictable and proportionate to the issue at stake and of taxpayers receiving value for the money they contribute to legal aid and the courts.

One explanation of the relative rise in expenditure suggests that it is inevitable. It is claimed that the judicial process is inherently highly labour-intensive so that

---

[1] From July 1995 in England and Wales, conditional fees can be agreed in personal injury cases, applications to the European Court of Human Rights, and insolvency cases. To date, it has been personal injury cases that have dominated this business (see Yarrow, 1998). The Law Reform (Miscellaneous Provisions) (Scotland) Act 1990 made similar provisions for solicitors and advocates in Scotland, using the term speculative basis as a reflection of the long-standing practice at the Scottish Bar. The White Paper *Modernising Justice* (1998) continues the pattern of reform by emphasizing the four areas of information, affordable legal services, law reform and improved management.

productivity gains which follow from the substitution of capital for labour, as found in manufacturing industry, cannot be achieved. This disadvantage cannot be offset by a fall in relative rates of remuneration of judges, lawyers and administrators which will depend on comparable opportunities in professional employment elsewhere in the economy, where labour's productivity and hence real wage is generally increasing. Thus, while growth in manufacturing costs will be offset by increases in productivity per head, costs to secure judicial output will rise even if no extra inputs are required (Baumol, 1996). There are some doubts about formulation of this hypothesis and the evidence supplied to substantiate it (Peacock, 1998), but even if it were true this would not preclude the strong possibility that, in an imperfect market for judicial services, better resource use could be achieved by more efficient management and, indeed, by removing the imperfections themselves.

This paper concentrates on the efficiency issue and, while concerned primarily with civil justice, many of the points made here carry over into the criminal field. As will be seen below, policy innovation is developing rapidly. While we attempt to present a comprehensive picture of the present state of the policy debate, our emphasis is on a general economic approach to the subject, an approach which we believe offers substantial insights. Despite the substantial differences between England and Wales and Scotland in respect of the content of civil law and procedure, efficiency is a common problem and methods for improving it have been traded between the two systems. References to both systems are freely made in what follows. Differences in legal terminology are explained in a Glossary, with the more unusual terms being italicized on their first appearance in the text.

The legal profession itself has recognized the need for reform. In both the Woolf Report (1995, 1996) and the Cullen Report (1995), major recommendations for change in current procedural arrangements are made. Indeed, some reforming action has already been taken (or is well underway, with the White Paper *Modernising Justice* (1998) in

12

England and Wales and *Access to Justice. Beyond the Year 2000* in Scotland). Reform is certainly not a novelty to any of the legal systems in the UK. For example, in England and Wales recent reform is evidenced by the Courts and Legal Services Act 1990 (permitting licensed conveyancers and implementing many of the recommendations of the 1988 Civil Justice Review under Sir Maurice Hodgson), and by Lord Mackays ending in 1995 of the Bar's monopoly regarding rights of audience in the higher courts. In Scotland, the Sheriff Court ordinary cause rules have recently been revised, thereby introducing simplified procedures and allowing sheriffs a much greater degree of discretion in case management. Also in Scotland, an optional procedure for personal injury cases has been introduced in the Court of Session. In a similar vein, an optional commercial cause procedure, involving a judge (initially Lord Penrose) dedicated to specific cases and empowered to intervene managerially in procedure, has successfully reached the end of an extensive pilot stage.

There is some concern, however, that, at least in Scotland, the process is currently stalled (Wadia, 1997). And in England and Wales, where reform is moving ahead, it is generally in the face of stiff resistance. In part, this may be ascribed to a confusion over objectives. A prime focus of discussion has been the perceived lengthy delay in the dispensation of civil justice (see below). Does this imply we require speedy justice? If so, accuracy may well suffer if speedier court decisions become more error-prone. There has also been an outcry regarding the expense of civil justice – both in terms of the civil legal aid bill and in terms of the prohibitive bills that can face a private litigant who lacks either legal aid, trade union backing or legal expenses insurance. In this context, considerable attention has been

given to the legal aid earnings of solicitors and counsel.[2] Could the same amount of justice be obtained more cheaply, or could more justice be on offer for the same expenditure? Any answer raises a further question concerning the costs and benefits to those who supply and demand justice, and to those called upon to finance it – the taxpayers (representing the community at large) or those paying directly for legal services.

Costs and Delay

In the statistical annex to the Woolf Report (1996) a survey based on a sample of the taxed costs of the winning side in over 2,000 High Court cases reveals surprisingly high costs. Across nine distinct categories of case (for example medical negligence and personal injury) where the claim value is under £12,500 the average or median costs of the winning side are invariably in excess of 100 per cent of the claim value. This proportion drops markedly, however, as the size of the claim rises. Thus for personal injury cases the median percentage falls to 41 per cent for claims between £12,500 and £25,000. It then drops to 28 per cent for those between £25,000 and £50,000 and eventually reaches 11 per cent for claims in excess of £250,000. This same survey also reveals delay, another cost consideration, to be a problem. The median duration from the date of instruction to conclusion for personal injury cases is fifty-four months. Medical negligence cases move even more slowly with a median duration of sixty-one months, while across the

---

[2] The House of Lords was recently asked to consider an appeal from a group of advocates whose fees in certain murder appeal cases were reduced on taxation. This included Mr Michael Mansfield, QC, whose request for fees had been reduced from £22,300 to £12,200 on taxation (*Sunday Times*, 18 June 1998). Part of the argument made on behalf of the barristers involved was that the Law Society references to appropriate legal aid rates in terms of the £120,000 per year earnings of NHS consultants were inappropriate. The appeal was denied on 15 October when the Law Lords declared that in the case of one bill, cut from a claimed £35,000 to a taxed £14,000, even the reduced figure was 'in our view generous'.

sample of cases as a whole the median duration is twenty-nine months.

Regulation

Part of the problem is that justice is a complex product. It is a professional service which for many infrequent users of the court system has to be bought as a matter of faith or trust (as a credence good) rather than being, as most commodities, purchased frequently and repeatedly (an experience or search good). Many professional services (for example accountancy, law and medicine) share such a characteristic and for this and other reasons the legal profession, as most others, is regulated (self-regulated, in fact) with respect to entry, personal behaviour and business conduct.

Precedent and Externality

A further complication arises because justice, as dispensed daily between rival parties in the courts, affects the interests of many others who may only be contemplating litigation. This spillover produces what economists term an externality which, for the individual, may be positive or negative, depending on the effect on a particular party or interest. The effect is readily understood in the case of precedents, or new rules, established by judges in novel cases. Unless subsequently overturned in a higher court, a precedent favouring a plaintiff may increase the probability of success for other plaintiffs and lower their costs, and *mutatis mutandis* raise the costs of defending such actions (but see section III below).

But there is also a wider and empirically more important spillover impact that relates to the notion of what Mnookin and Kornhauser (1979) label bargaining in the shadow of the law. In addition to those caught up in the formal legal system, the behaviour of parties engaged in disputes, and indeed of those for whom no dispute is in hand but whose behaviour might engender a dispute, is affected by the civil justice system. The prospect of ending up in a court room with the generally accepted prospect of liability, damages, and costs leads all individuals and enterprises to take a higher

level of care, thereby avoiding many disputes. The knowledge of what might happen if a dispute ends up in court also facilitates entry into voluntary (or at least non-judicial) resolution of many disputes that do arise. It is worth remembering that even among the cases set down or filed in court, only around 5 per cent ever come before a judge for final judgement or proof. The remainder settle by mutual agreement – but with the settlement parameters defined by expectations of what would happen in court.[3]

Thus in evaluating the civil justice system or in recommending change, it is important to bear in mind that it is part of a large dispute-resolution process, and changes will have potentially significant knock-on effects elsewhere. In this sense, looking at court-room procedure in isolation is not at all appropriate. As the externality example demonstrates, a further complication is that there are very obvious and potentially serious distributional questions involved. If poor people are to be allowed to have their grievances addressed in court, then they must be provided with resources. Where to draw the line, in terms of which people are to be deemed in need of support and the extent of the support to provide any one person in a particular case, then becomes a value judgement. These distributional questions tend to distract policy makers from focusing on the efficiency aspect, and, indeed, often threaten to derail reform. Our analysis here focuses first on efficiency before turning to the distributional issue, which we treat as an important but distinct problem. Our conclusion is that there is scope in the system for substantial experimentation with procedural reform, and that as much as possible should be done to encourage the development of a cafeteria-style civil justice system with improved information flows and

---

[3] This is in marked contrast with the experience in the continental inquisitorial system where pre-trial settlement is much lower. In France, for example, the figure is typically around 25 per cent (Doriat and Deffains, 1998).

provision for innovations such as cost-capping and risk-sharing between legal representatives and clients.

In section II of the paper, we look at the general market characteristics of the supply of and demand for civil justice by examining the product specification. Then, in section III, we take up the notion of externality and examine its implications for reform. In section IV we address the various possible remedies for the market imperfection arising out of the externality, while in section V we turn to the vexed issue of distribution. The paper concludes in section VI with some suggestions regarding reform strategies that may guide policy makers in this area.

II. Product Specification

As discussed in the Introduction, civil justice is a service, and that service is dispute resolution. The formal civil justice system is part of a spectrum of dispute resolution mechanisms that are at work throughout the economy. But in many ways it is the cogwheel that drives the whole system. It represents the court of last resort – when all other forms of dispute resolution fail to bring the parties together in a mutually satisfactory way, it stands ready to bring closure to any competent dispute. In addition it possesses enforcement power to ensure compliance with its ruling (*diligence*), and it possesses a rule-setting attribute in the form of precedents and procedural rules.

All the other commonly used forms of dispute resolution depend in some way on this formal element. These alternatives work only because the courts operate in a particular way in allocating and enforcing liability, damages and costs according to well-understood rules. This influence on the operation of each of these particular alternatives is not generally acknowledged explicitly. Furthermore, whether it is breach of contract, tort-based harm, or marital dissolution, behaviour that is likely to result in a dispute will be influenced by the parameters set in the civil courts. For example, given the prospect of an injured party being able to seek redress, with recourse if need be to the courts, individuals and enterprises are induced to behave in a more considerate manner. The rules set explicitly and implicitly by the courts also remove the uncertainty about which party is to bear any risk, and thereby allow appropriate action to be taken to mitigate that risk.

Demand

There are, in general, two types of purchaser of civil legal services. The first is the one-time buyer for whom the costs

of obtaining and evaluating information on the range and quality of legal services available can be high. Purchases are, therefore, typically made on faith, and for this type of buyer legal service is a credence good, where it can be argued that some form of third-party regulation is beneficial. The second type is the professional or repeat buyer, who may be a business enterprise. Here there is ample opportunity to gain information on the nature of suppliers and to make informed purchases based on experience. To these buyers, legal services are an experience good, where the normal stricture of *caveat emptor* leads to an efficient outcome. Thus the Automobile Association (AA), with a high volume of members' cases requiring legal representation but with these cases being of a fairly standard and well-specified nature, could enter into block contracts with solicitors around the country whereby a set price could be agreed for a given standard of service in a set number of cases.

It can be argued that, even among the one-time buyers, social networks and reputation (not to mention brand-labelling) can overcome the information asymmetry that exists between lawyer and client, thereby improving the client's prospect of obtaining good service.[4] But, be that as it may, it is for this credence-good group that the legal professions justify regulations regarding entry and conduct. Regulation comes from the relevant Law Society in the case of solicitors, from the Bar Council for barristers, and from the Faculty of Advocates for advocates.

Regulation

The market for legal services is imperfectly competitive. As explained above, lawyers – advocates, barristers and solicitors – are self regulated, private suppliers of services. Entry to the professions is not open to all, but carefully

---

[4] In economists' jargon, labelling or reputation helps avoid what has come to be known as the 'market for lemons' problem that tends to arise in such situations whereby poor quality products drive out better quality, so spoiling the market.

controlled by stipulation of educational and professional qualifications as well as defined practical experience. Thus, Baldwin (1997) explains how in England and Wales aspiring solicitors are required to secure a recognized law degree or to pass the Common Professional Examination/Diploma (CPE) in law before taking the Legal Practice Course (LPC); on successful completion of this they must secure a training contract with a qualified solicitor, during which time a Professional Skills Course (PSC) must be completed. The Bar Council administers a similar set of admission procedures for aspiring barrister – a qualifying law degree or CPE, Bar Vocational Course (BVC) and a twelve-month period of pupillage after which a position in a Chambers (tenancy) may be sought.

Once accepted by the profession, each type of practitioner is subject to a code of professional conduct. In addition, both the capacity (number of courtrooms and judges) and admission charges (court fees) to their most formal operating arena, the courts, are determined by an administrative procedure – either directly by the government or through some quasi-governmental agency such as the Lord Chancellor's Department or the Scottish Courts Administration.

Supplier-Induced Demand and Collusion

For the uninformed buyer, there remains the problem of supplier-induced demand,[5] whereby the legal practitioner is in the position of both recommending the quantity and quality of product to be purchased and simultaneously supplying it (and thereby possibly engaging in the practice of fee-building). There are clear principal–agent problems here. This is one reason that can be advanced for accepting substantial regulation of the profession in order that behaviour can be policed effectively. Regulation, however, brings its own problems owing to the potential it creates for

---

[5] Sometimes less contentiously labelled 'provider moral hazard'. See Bevan (1996).

collusive behaviour and restrictive practices. Collusive behaviour would arise, for example, were all solicitors to agree to refrain from competing on price by using standard fee schedules to price their services. In conveyancing, the use of such mandatory fee schedules or fixed-fee scales was in operation in Scotland until 1985 (in England and Wales until 1974). Self-imposed restrictions on recruitment of new trainees,[6] or on price and non-price competition through advertising, or on organisational form (for instance multi-disciplinary practices) could all result from collusive behaviour.

Deregulation

In many ways there has been a remarkable deregulation of the profession over recent years (Stephen and Love, 1999). For example, following a 1976 investigation by the Monopolies and Mergers Commission (MMC) and subsequent government pressure, by the mid-1980s advertising by solicitors was permitted – although within certain bounds and generally stopping short of anything approaching the unthinkable 'touting for business'. Since 1985 solicitors have been permitted to operate in a corporate form, and since 1990 they may form partnerships with non-solicitors in England. Since 1977, Queens Counsel have been permitted to revise pleadings directly rather than through a junior, and to appear without junior counsel. Furthermore, the idea that any junior counsel (whose involvement the senior continues to have a right to insist upon should this be felt necessary) should automatically be paid a fee at a rate of two-thirds that of the senior has also been swept away. However, advocates in Scotland retain the legal right to conduct a case without any regard to the wishes of the client and, on the grounds of public policy, the

---

[6] Baldwin (1997, p. 23) relates how in 1995 the Law Society investigated the possibility of regulating the number of places on Legal Practice Courses (LPC) and, hence, entry to the profession. Unsurprisingly, it was advised that this would be illegal (a restraint of trade).

advocate is deemed not liable for any wrong advice in law, negligence and mistakes.

While both barristers and solicitors in England and Wales enjoy considerable immunity from negligence suits regarding their court work, their position is now less strong in the area of non-litigious and pre-trial work. In addition, since 1990 wasted costs orders allow the court to make legal agents personally liable for costs that arise out of negligent or obstructive conduct by the agent (Zander, 1996, p. 428). But, as a recent paper by Reeves (1998) on the system of Queens Counsel in England and Wales argues, the professions are still subject to criticism regarding restrictive practices. Reeves's arguments include claims regarding the closed nature of the procedure of appointment to silk, that becoming a silk is the main route into the ranks of the higher judiciary, and that the elevation to silk facilitates both the restrictive practice of using juniors and the charging of higher fees.

Apart from parties directly involved, right of audience in court by any other than an advocate, barrister or solicitor is severely restricted. There is provision in Scotland for cases under the Debtors (Scotland) Act 1987 and other *summary cause* procedures in the Sheriff Courts to allow representation by a layman friend of the party. But here the court has to be satisfied that the person is qualified, and the practice seems mostly to be used as a device for allowing trainees to appear. Since 1991, it has been possible for solicitors in both England and Wales and in Scotland, after satisfying certain training courses and other hurdles set by their respective Law Societies, to gain right of audience in the higher courts,[7] previously the exclusive domains of barristers and advocates who had to be briefed by solicitors, thereby, it is alleged, adding to costs.

---

[7] These higher courts being the Crown Court and the High Court in England and Wales, and the Court of Session and the High Court in Scotland.

Perhaps the greatest step forward in England and Wales regarding alternative representation has been the provision under the Courts and Legal Services Act 1990 for non-solicitors to provide conveyancing services (through licensed conveyancers). While there has been substantial entry to this new profession, Stephen and Love (1996) find little evidence of downward pressure on prices, although Domberg and Sherr (1995) are more positive in their appraisal. In 1990, a Scottish Conveyancing and Executry Services Board was set up under the Law Reform (Miscellaneous Provisions) (Scotland) Act 1990, but by 1992 it had been suspended in the face of the (then) housing-market collapse, having made no impact. By and large, therefore, conveyancing in Scotland is left to solicitors. Indeed, the very Scottish cartel-like exclusive arrangements among solicitors to advertise and sell properties (for example the Edinburgh Solicitors' Property Centre) were recently investigated by the Office of Fair Trading for restricted practices and exonerated.

Judges and Court Fees

While, in most markets, market forces ensure that any upturn in demand brings forth an increase in supply, in the area of legal services the determination of overall judicial capacity (a key feature of the system) is an administrative decision of the government. In England and Wales there are 96 High Court Judges (up from 78 in 1985), 539 Circuit Judges (371 in 1985) 1207 Recorders and Assistant Recorders (992 in 1985), and 337 District Judges (189 in 1985). In Scotland, the Court of Session currently has 26 full-time judges (up from 23 in 1985), known as Senators of the College of Justice and also responsible for criminal business in the High Court, and the Sheriff Courts have 6 sheriff principals, 109 sheriffs,[8]

---

[8] These statistics are taken from *The Lord Chancellor's Department Judicial Statistics for England and Wales, Scottish Court Service, Annual Report and Accounts 1996–97, and Civil Judicial Statistics Scotland.* Thanks are also due to Mrs Hardie and Mr Ritchie of the Scottish Court Service for help with some of these statistics.

and 119 temporary sheriffs[9] (up from 6 sheriff principals, 88 sheriffs, and 61 temporary sheriffs in 1985). Growth in judicial capacity is, therefore, clearly a reality, but the process by which it occurs is not market-responsive.

Court fees are levied for all court business and there has been a marked move over recent years to ensure that fees are set at a level that covers court operating costs (including judges' salaries). For example, in the Scottish higher courts, targets of covering at least 80 per cent of all costs in 1996–97 and 90 per cent in 1997–98 were both successfully attained.[10] One major scheduling consideration peculiar to Scotland is that civil justice, in general, is placed as a residual claimant in the system owing to the priority given to criminal cases in allocating judicial resources. This priority is due to the 80-day and 110-day rules in Scots Law whereby detained suspects[11] must be tried or released within that period (one-year for those at freedom but charged).

Lawyers

In terms of the supply of lawyers, there is a widely held view on both sides of the Atlantic that the market is kept artificially in short supply, so ensuring practitioners unusually high earnings. In fact, careful scrutiny of the data for the USA by Rosen (1992) shows that lawyers on average earn a level of pay that is commensurate with the training period that is necessary for qualification and the hours per week that lawyers work. Figures on entry to the professions also show that there has been remarkably easy entry over recent decades – notwithstanding the fear that supply could

---

[9] Since November 1999, the legality of such temporary sheriff posts has been questioned and they are at present in suspension.

[10] These fact are revealed in the 1996–97 and the 1997–98 Annual Accounts of the Scottish Court Service. The higher courts are the Sheriff Courts and the Court of Session.

[11] The 80-day rule pertains to the time limit for an indictment on a person in custody under petition (solemn procedure).

be constrained by manipulation or control over training places.[12]

Recent figures[13] on the profitability of legal practices among solicitors in Scotland show that for profit-sharing partners the median level of annual profit per partner was £44,934 with an interquartile range from £30,683 to £62,113. Of course not everyone reaches the level of partner. Figures from the Law Society[14] reveal that average annual earnings among male (female) solicitors are: assistant solicitors £24,000 (£23,000); salaried partner £40,200 (£33,000); and equity partners £50,520 (£40,180). What often catches the headlines is the earnings, or putative earnings, of superstars. It is true that there is a remarkably wide variation in earnings within the legal profession. This is, as Rosen (1981) explains, simply a manifestation of talent commanding its market rate. If there is one outstanding barrister (say) who can deliver a 10 per cent higher chance of winning than any alternative barrister, and if there is a net £1 million at stake, then it is easy to see how that barrister could command a premium fee of some £100,000.

Judges' salaries[15] (usually taken to represent the high end of the salary range for the non-'superstars') do not suggest unusually high remuneration when compared with other

---

[12] See Baldwin (1997), for a comprehensive discussion of regulation of the legal profession in England and Wales. In one example (p. 68) he quotes the 2400 applicants for places on the Bar Vocational Course at the Inns of Court School of Law (one of eight such providers), where some 883 completed the course in 1994, of whom only 657 secured a pupillage by October 1994. Set against the 500 or so tenancies that are expected to be available in any year, then professional entry is certainly not unchecked. That said, some of what is going on here is undoubtedly quality screening (for example acceptance on courses and admission to training places), and some may reflect market demand (for example available tenancies in Chambers).

[13] See McCutcheon (1998).

[14] As reported in *The Times*, 19 October 1998, p. 10.

[15] Judicial salaries can be found at the LCD web site: http://www.open.gov.uk/lcd.

senior responsible jobs. In 1998 a High Court Judge or one of the less senior (Outer House) Court of Session Judges earned £117,752 per year. The more numerous sheriffs earn £88,077, and district judges earn £70,820. But judges' positions offer a substantially more secure stream of earnings (not to mention pension) than that enjoyed by most barristers or advocates.

Other Participants in the Legal Process

The court system also depends on other actors, not least among whom are witnesses and juries. In England and Wales, since as long ago as the Administration of Justice Act 1933, judges had discretion as to whether or not jury trials should be allowed in civil cases. Over the intervening years the scope of jury trials has been further limited. Civil jury trials now number less than 400 or so cases per year, and are generally restricted to defamation and fraud cases. In Scotland, where jury trials were reintroduced in 1815 to come into line with the then English practice, juries[16] may still be used in the Court of Session in claims for personal injuries, libel and defamation. While juries sometimes sit in certain personal injury cases, they are extremely rare as most judges disallow them if there is any complexity – for example a pension issue – involved. Juries do not represent a serious expense in most civil cases.

Witnesses in civil cases tend to be of the expert kind and are, consequently remunerated at market rates for their service. So while the time of witnesses and juries represents an important social cost in terms of criminal justice, it creates less of a problem in civil justice (save to the extent that the use of rival experts may permit a prolongation of the procedure as a consequence of strategic manoeuvring by one or both sides).

---

[16] Civil juries in Scotland comprise twelve persons as opposed to the fifteen used in criminal trials under solemn procedure. Jury trials have been abolished in the Sheriff Courts (since 1980), and in the Outer House of the Court of Session they number only some four or five per year.

Alternative Sources of Supply

Thus the state has a monopoly on court rooms and judges, and the legal professions through their regulatory bodies have scope for restrictive practices concerning admission to the professions, membership of the professions, and the way in which the court system works. As with all monopolies, however, competition may be stimulated by the provision of near-substitutes in the product market. In this case, private negotiation between parties or their agents may suffice to resolve any dispute – no formality is needed. A halfway house between this unstructured atmosphere and the regulated procedure-bound court room can be found in alternative dispute resolution (ADR).[17] Under this arrangement it is possible to choose a quasi-judicial mode of arbitration by a third party under mutually agreed procedural rules, or, alternatively, to have much more open-ended and party-driven form of mediation where the third party appears as a facilitator rather than an adjudicator.

Mediation is favoured in some US jurisdictions as a compulsory step prior to formal court proceedings. Although the idea of mediation finds much support in the UK, with various groupings such as ACCORD (under the Law Society of Scotland), CALM (Comprehensive Accredited Lawyer Mediators), CEDR (Centre for Dispute Resolution), the Mediation Bureau, and many other agencies all offering mediation services, only a small part of court business is diverted to mediation. Family law is the major exception here, as mediation is set to play an increasingly important role in preventing marital break-ups and in easing any child-custody decisions that do have to be made. In its proposed reforms of legal aid, the White Paper *Modernising Justice* (1998) makes specific allowance for support of mediation services in both family cases and, indeed, in other appropriate civil cases (3.13). The reparation-type business

---

[17] Editor's note: alternative dispute resolution is discussed in more detail in Bruce Benson's Commentary on this paper, pp. 69–96.

may be more likely to involve mediation as a first step after a recent decision in England and Wales that will allow legal aid expenditures to be used to support mediation. Hitherto legal aid could only be used to pay for the more formal court related procedures.

In general, the submission of a dispute to arbitration has the effect of excluding the courts. Subsequent appeal by one party to the court will have no effect if the matter is judged to be contractual (either in the *ex-ante* sense of a contract clause or in the *ex-post* sense of a post-dispute private agreement between the parties). The arbitrator's award is generally final and cannot be appealed to a court, being open to challenge only on procedural grounds. The courts will, however, assist with the enforcement of arbitrators' awards.

The legal professions have not been slow to move into these areas and, indeed, it could be argued that such activity has always comprised an important part of their work, albeit not always formally labelled as alternative dispute resolution. The important point is that the finding of a solution in all of these alternative situations presupposes the existence of the formal court mechanism. Much as the central bank, the Bank of England, stands behind the UK monetary system guaranteeing its probity as banker-of-last-resort, so the court system stands as an arbiter-of-last-resort.

Choice of Procedure

The resolution of many disputes can be achieved in a way that leaves both sides better off. Failure to agree can, in the jargon of the negotiation literature, leave money on the table. This is particularly true when the dispute or prospect of dispute inhibits a mutually beneficial trade or commercial or other relationship. Each mode of dispute resolution has its own value-added. Value-added arises from procedures that allow new facts to emerge or different appraisals of solutions to be made. Any value-added will, of course, be net of such transaction costs as are introduced by the dispute-resolution mechanism. Indeed, in choosing among the various modes of dispute resolution, lower costs will prove a

29

prime attraction in many cases. It can be argued that the emergence of ADR in recent years is an indication of competitive forces in the system. A major dimension of this competition is the determination of the nature of the procedural rules under which cases progress through the system.

From this perspective, Lord Woolf's (1996) proposals that cases be allocated to one of three tracks (small claims, fast track, and multi-track) based on the value of claim involved[18] can be seen as product innovation. These proposals, which come into force on 26 April 1999 encourage active managerial intervention by judges in an effort to move cases more expeditiously through the system. As time, or delay, can be expensive this must be applauded. But there are non-trivial resource implications owing to the substantial up-front input of judicial time that is required. A higher level of judge, the Designated Civil Judge, has been created to oversee this new aspect of the system. In addition, it should be remembered that, in any case, around 95 per cent of all civil reparation cases settle before they reach trial or proof. As the extra and early judicial input will be reflected in court fees, it might be better if an element of choice were allowed in any fast-track/multi-track system of case management. If the two parties disagree, then there could be a judge-led process of determining the appropriate procedural track.[19] Efforts at such active judicial intervention in case management can be traced back to the 1953 Evershed Committee and the resulting summons for directions, which were generally recognized to have failed (Zander, 1996, p. 77). The explicit provision of Designated Civil Judges and the commitment to introducing new information technology[20]

---

[18] With this division will come procedural restrictions, for example, no cost-shifting in small claims, and substantial judicial involvement in case of management for fast-track and multi-track.

[19] A suggestion made by Zuckerman (1995, p. 171).

[20] The White Paper, *Modernising Justice* (1998), sections 4.5 and 4.6.

suggest that reform may have more chance of having a significant impact this time around.

Lord Cullen (1995) made related case-management proposals for the Outer House of the Court of Session, but suggested that track allocation be based on the complexity of the case rather than the damages involved. The reaction to the Cullen Report has been one of great caution. In fact, it is tempting to recall Hume's words when he described the disappointing public reaction to the publication of his *Treatise of Human Nature*, namely that 'It fell dead-born from the press, without reaching such distinction, as even to excite a murmur from the zealots'.[21] A kinder interpretation might be that the legal establishment in Scotland has had time to benefit from the results of a study of case management in the USA by the Rand Corporations Institute of Civil Justice (Gill, 1997). This study suggests that case management is extremely demanding on judicial time and effort, particularly in the early stages of litigation (after which many cases settle out of court).

While advocating a liberalization of procedure, we should enter a cautionary note. Choice of procedural complexity would, in our view, afford participants the possibility of lower-cost dispute resolution. It would be naive, of course, not to expect each side to try for the arrangement that is to its own particular advantage. In general, it could be expected that mutually advantageous accommodations could be found, and, failing that, in the absence of any agreement there would always be the default arrangement. The possibility of increased transaction costs through forum shopping as happens in the USA does not by itself deny the possibility of lower overall costs. Finally, while procedural choice and reform can affect the relative costs of the various modes, lowering transaction costs, for instance through reducing delay, is not always synonymous with increased value for money. Peacock (1994) makes the analogy with a symphony orchestra striving for efficiency by playing its

---

[21] Hume's disappointed reaction was premature, as history was to reveal.

pieces at twice the appropriate speed, thereby destroying the product! Efficiency gains can be illusory in cheaper channels of dispute resolution if what is produced leaves the parties worse off.

Risk and Uncertainty

Although we have emphasized the state's monopoly in the provision of judicial capacity and the regulated nature of other legal services, there is, as we have indicated above, always a choice. In terms of resolving a grievance a party can variously: forget it (allow the grievance to lapse); resolve matters privately; use an agent but not the court (ADR, for example.); or go to court. Only in this last is the consumer directly exposed to the impact of the regulated court system. Indeed, the extent of demand for less formal channels will depend in part on the degree of congestion, delay and expense involved in utilizing the formal sector. The knowledge that any dispute, should one arise, can end up in a formal court-room colours the way that all upstream negotiations are handled.

One problem in taking formal legal action is that the costs are not known at the outset. It is like buying a product in a shop with little or no idea of what the final bill will be. Legal costs come in various forms: court fees; expert witness fees; lawyers' fees; the possibility of being held liable for the other party's costs; delay; and strategic behaviour of the other party (including opportunistic use of *discovery provisions*, extravagant case preparation, and so on). Many of these costs are not pre-set but depend on the development of the case, the decisions taken by one's own legal representatives, and the decisions taken by the opponent's legal representatives. Thus, the other side in the dispute can increase the resource allocated to case preparation or use of expert witnesses, or quality (expense) of legal counsel, and this will call for similar if not matching expenditures. That response in itself might then induce a further escalation,

and so on in an upward spiral that brings no real advantage to either side.[22]

At the moment, the typical legal contract that exists between clients and their lawyers looks very like the cost-plus style of contract that has traditionally produced huge cost overruns in the defence industry. The client is exposed to the expenditure of his or her own legal representatives (while these expenses may be reported as they arise, they are generally only roughly estimated in advance). But, the client is also exposed to the rival's legal bill should the verdict go the wrong way, or at least the audited part of it (*inter-partes* costs, those judged absolutely necessary for conducting the case and awarded against the loser). Given that for at least one class of consumer the experience is relatively rare, then one can expect some risk aversion. By contrast the legal representatives, this being their work day in and day out, can spread any risk over a large number of cases. It might consequently appear that there is scope here for a mutually advantageous form of contracting that shifts the risk to the party best able to bear it. The Lord Chancellor, encouraged by Sir Peter Middleton's (1997) report, is currently considering the use of fixed-fee contracts in England and Wales. Consultation on the principles regarding civil court fees ended on 1 May 1998, and concrete proposals are expected soon.

Negotiating with one's legal representative over price or method of remuneration to apply in each case is difficult at present. Indeed, certain fee contracts are currently not allowed, and competing aggressively on the basis of price is explicitly discouraged by the Law Society. It has long been possible in Scotland for an advocate to agree to operate on a speculative basis, whereby no fee is charged in the event of defeat but a proportionately higher fee (such as a 50 per cent premium on the fee computed on hours of work) is charged if successful. To date, this has not been commonly used, although, as discussed above, the green light given by

---

[22] See Main (1997, p. 6) for more detail.

recent legislation to the use of a similar type of conditional fee in England and Wales and to allow solicitors in Scotland to operate on a speculative basis may well change this.[23] The conditional fee (no-win/no-fee) has now been in operation since July 1995 and is generally judged a success (Yarrow, 1998). Originally available only for personal injury cases, in July 1998 the government extended coverage to all types of civil case except those involving family law. Insurance against having to pay the legal expenses of the defence, in the eventuality of the plaintiffs case being lost is now available from Accident Line Protect (set up by the Law Society) and Litigation Protection (a private company) in England and Wales, and from Compensure (set up by the Law Society of Scotland) in Scotland.

The more full-blooded risk-shifting variant used in the USA, namely the contingent fee, is not allowed in the UK. That said, some commentators, such as Walker (1997, p. 381), are of the view that nothing exists in law to prevent this arrangement in Scotland, and Middleton (1997) has recommended active reconsideration of its introduction in England and Wales. In Scotland, at least one individual, acting in a corporate rather than a personal or professional capacity, has exploited the fact that a non-professional person may advance funds to carry out litigation in return for receiving a share of the recovery or damages if successful. Assuming an interest of this kind in a case is known as *champerty* (Painter, 1995; Tan, 1990) and was traditionally debarred to professional lawyers in the UK owing to the bias it may impart to professional judgement. Contingency fees are explicitly excepted from champerty doctrine in the USA

---

[23] The Law Reform (Miscellaneous Provisions) (Scotland) Act 1990 makes the arrangement explicit for solicitors in Scotland. In a similar fashion so does the July 4 1995 changes made by the then Lord Chancellor, Lord Mackay, under the Courts and Legal Services Act 1990. The success fee cannot exceed 100 per cent of the usual fee and most agents agree not to charge more than 25 per cent of the quantum of damages recovered.

(where the exemption was ratified by the Supreme Court as long ago as 1877).

Third-Party Sources of Costs

Self-funding aside, demand is strongly affected by the prospect of someone else picking up the tab. Usually this prospect (other than courtesy of the judicially imposed consequence of the British loser-pays rule) comes about through legal aid, trade union backing, or legal expenses insurance. In the last two, the person can be regarded as making an efficient allocation of resources in the sense that the agent pays the expected cost of the expense beforehand, in a risk-pooling mechanism common to most insurance schemes. There are obvious self-selection problems and moral hazard problems of the type that arise in any insurance situation, but given that both the insurance company and the trade union are professional organizations then contract design arrangements such as screening programmes and co-insurance should minimize these difficulties.[24]

With legal aid, however, there is a more serious allocation problem. In its original form, legal aid placed qualified (means-tested) individuals in a free or zero-price situation. Strict means testing and recently instituted reforms involving moves toward co-payments eliminate some of this difficulty, but legal aid clients are undoubtedly presented with stronger incentives to litigate than other citizens (particularly those in the middle-income range). The position of a legal aid litigant is further strengthened by the deviation from the English rule in the event of such a plaintiff losing – they are not generally held liable for the other side's costs (save at the discretion of the court). This advantage gives the plaintiff with legal aid a substantial advantage in pre-trial bargaining. Recognized as an

---

[24] In the past, insurance companies have found themselves constrained in this field by EU law guaranteeing individual freedom of choice of solicitor, and by certain aspects of champerty and the related concept of maintenance. See Rickman and Fenn (1998, p. 217).

oppressive effect in a recent Lord Chancellor's Department report,[25] the intention revealed in the White Paper *Modernising Justice* (1998) is that lawyers will share risks with clients under conditional fee arrangements, and that clients with substantial housing equity may, indeed, find themselves liable for costs. Moves in England and Wales to divert all Legal Aid Board personal injury cases (with the exception of medical malpractice) to a conditional fee arrangement, plus the encouragement given to the franchising or block purchase of legal aid, and the possible development of more broadly based Community Legal Service should counter some of these incentive problems. There is also a White Paper (1998) commitment that the costs of insurance (Accident Line Protect, Compensure, etc.) be recoverable from the other side by the successful plaintiff as a disbursement. The success fee component of the conditional fee will also be recoverable along with other taxed costs.

In Scotland, the recent government position paper on civil legal aid, *Access to Justice. Beyond the Year 2000*, suggests that more lawyers may be employed directly by the Scottish Legal Aid Board (SLAB), to work in advice centres providing a first layer of legal advice that might go some way to separating the agency function (of prescribing the possible cure to the problem) from the service function (of delivering that cure) – the principal–agent problem that is often cited as leading to supplier-induced demand in medicine, the law and other professions. Moves on funding and fixed fees are less well advanced in civil legal aid in Scotland, as the argument regarding inefficiency is rebutted with statistics showing that the Scottish Legal Aid Board recovers (out of damages awards, fee awards, and client contributions) over 80 per cent of all expenses relating to reparation cases. This is taken as evidence that the merits test is already working. Under the merits test, solicitors are meant to estimate the chances of the case prevailing if it were to go to trial or proof

---

[25] *Access to Justice with Conditional Fees*. A Lord Chancellor's Department Consultation Paper, March 1998, para. 3.4.

as being reasonable, before applying for legal aid on behalf of their client. Lord Irvine has suggested that the merit test should be strengthened to stipulate a 75 per cent likelihood of success as a funding condition.[26] The White Paper *Modernising Justice* (1998) does not go as far as stating an explicit probability hurdle but does refer to whether a reasonable person able to fund the case with his or her own money would be prepared to pursue it (3.25). While this is qualified by public policy considerations, it is clear that the civil legal aid system is in for substantial reform. Rather than rationing access, it might be better to try to think of ways that can encourage as many people as possible to have access to dispute-resolution facilities of the courts. Innovative procedure, funding mechanisms and fee charging can all play a part.

Other Sources of Demand

There are other more macro causes of demand for civil justice. These are primarily societal in nature, and include the rise of so-called dysfunctional families, and the increased prevalence of employment rights that have accompanied the extensive passage of statute law covering the labour market. This last development includes trade union law as, while there are now fewer trade union rights, somewhat paradoxically there are many more trade union laws on the statute book. This macro dimension is additional to the economic factors such as rising incomes and rising education already mentioned. A process of changing tastes and social mores is in train. This marked social change has also encouraged civil litigation. In general, we now live in a more assertive and rights-conscious society. The general attitude among the public has changed and people are much more likely to sue for their rights.

---

[26] See Lord Irvine's address to the Solicitors' Annual Conference at Cardiff (18 October 1997). This change would require legislation and will be unnecessary if there is a major move to conditional fees, although it will still have a bearing on family work.

Product Specification

We therefore have a complex product whose quality and characteristics are difficult to ascertain before purchase and, partly in consequence, whose supply is heavily regulated. Demand for this product is a derived demand, resting on the demand for dispute resolution. Changing social mores and the increased complexity of modern life seem set to drive this demand upwards. It is at the interface between supply and demand, where the price is set and the quantity and quality agreed, that seems to offer most scope for product innovation. In both England and Wales and in Scotland, there are initiatives being taken by the government to change the legal aid system. These changes will have a direct influence on the way all civil cases are dealt with. In addition, there are general procedural changes being made – particularly, but not exclusively, in case management – which are likely to have a significant impact. They demonstrate that change is possible. Change and innovation could also be encouraged in a more general sense, for example between client and lawyer in contracting for service, or between lawyer and lawyer in agreeing procedure. But this would require much more information and much more attention to freedom to contract than appears to exist at the moment.

III. Externalities

If the volume of litigation were the sole measure of the benefit to society of the resolution of disputes, then there would be little to distinguish judicial services from the provision of other goods and services in the market. Those unwilling to pay for the services could be denied them (the mechanism usually known as the exclusion principle) and the benefits arising from the resolution of a dispute would be confined to that particular individual case (known as rival consumption). Even if the courts were endowed with a monopoly, it is possible to devise schemes which would simulate competitive pricing, a matter which has received some attention from economists.[27] But the claim that there are benefits other than those accruing to litigants using court services must lead one to look more closely at the process of dispute resolution and the case for government intervention.

A common argument which supports the case that benefits exist other than those which accrue to litigants in court is that precedents are created (Fiss, 1984). In principle, the establishment of precedent in disputes may reduce uncertainty in the minds of subsequent litigants and their advisers about how to proceed with a case. Precedents are constantly evolving as a result of new situations which arise from often rapid changes in economic and social conditions. However, whether precedents have the power to reduce transaction costs to litigants to any major extent has yet to

---

[27] Gravelle (1996) has considered this particular point. Smith (1776, book V, i. 6) was aware of the need to provide judges with a financial incentive to expedite justice. Other writers such as Benson (1997), Bernstein (1992), Friedman (1979), and Landes and Posner (1979) have examined the possibility of private systems of law enforcement and adjudication.

be empirically tested and is often disputed in principle. Measurement would require the calculation of the amount of dispute expenses (lawyers' fees being an obvious one) that are avoided when a precedent clarifies what had until then been a disputed area of the law. One would also have to add the efficiency gains obtained through operating the economy under the new rule. It is necessary to bear in mind, however, that only a tiny proportion of judgements ever leads to anything approaching a precedent. The small number of cases that are appealed, and the even smaller number that result in a judgement of material significance to the interpretation of the law, bear witness to this fact. The vast proportion of judgements resolve purely private disputes whereby no third party is any the wiser or better off.

In any case, a more empirically robust argument can be made for the manner in which the courts influence the process by which all disputes are resolved. The fact that the courts operate in a more or less recognizable and predictable way and with a known standard of accuracy is likely to encourage out-of-court settlement, which is clearly less expensive. As it happens, a large proportion of cases in Scotland, England and Wales, North America, and elsewhere, perhaps exceeding 95 per cent in most years, are settled between filing and a court appearance for judgement or proof, although admittedly the settlement often occurs only at the door of the court itself. The influence of the courts extends back into encouragement to disputing parties to settle grievances without going near a lawyer's office. The influence of the courts extends even to increasing the confidence of individuals to enter contracts that offer mutually advantageous gains, but clarifying what is likely to happen in the event of one party or other not complying with all details of the agreement. The courts through their actions and decisions also persuade all actors in the economy to behave with due regard to the necessity to exercise a reasonable amount of care, bearing in mind the costs of litigation that will ensue in the event of harm being caused. In short, a socially efficient (but not zero) level of litigation encourages beneficial economic activity.

While we argue above that ADR and the like provide a competitive source of dispute resolution that tends to undermine any attempt by the formal system to exploit its monopoly power, at the same time there are disadvantages to private-channel dispute resolution.[28] The public is deprived of information, the deterrence of negative behaviour is made less likely, there is no information gained as there would be from a public trial, and there is no public exposure of either party. In addition, the very secrecy of ADR procedures opens up the possibility that settlements contrary to the public interest may be permitted (for example involving monopolistic exploitation of third parties or a restraint of trade). Of course, the public is not concerned (or not primarily so) with the social purpose of litigation. The decision to proceed to law or ADR is based primarily on private preference and private calculus as to the costs and benefits. But a court system with lower transaction costs will place downward pressure on dispute-resolution costs throughout the system. As long as accuracy is not disproportionately weakened, then there should be an increase in value-added, both in terms of disposing with court cases and in terms of expanding the margin of disputes that are resolved in one venue or another) and an extension of the margin of harm that is redressed or avoided. This then allows more mutually advantageous contracts and exchanges to be effected.

It is more difficult to judge whether these arguments are sufficiently strong to justify large public subsidy to the civil justice system. Such subsidy in a system that is still quite heavily regulated is always in danger of capture by vested interests within the system. What does seem clear is that increased competitiveness and increased flexibility in contracting offer gains to society that extend well beyond those identified as directly consuming the services of the civil justice system.

---

[28] Editor's note: see the discussion of ADR in Bruce Benson's Commentary on this paper, pp. 69–96.

IV. Remedies for Market Imperfection

In addition to the positive externality discussed above, the imperfection in this market concerns its regulated nature. With an administratively determined number of judges and court rooms, and a complex bureaucratic process of determining procedural rules (and hence product specification), it is very easy for this market to under-perform. We argue in this subsection that increased information, choice and product diversity should all be used in shaping a way forward. It is clear that a court system that uses resources efficiently is desirable. But efficient need not mean the lowest unit cost per court case. The system might be very cheap but so hopeless at determining fault as to be little better than a lottery (Main, 1997; Peacock, 1998). In that case economic activity and private contracting would be discouraged.

At the same time, an extremely high unit-cost system could offer an unerring accuracy in determining the truth (although a problem arises in cases where the concept of truth is elusive). Such a system would provide the parties with an incentive to settle out of court and would provide all parties *ex ante* with the confidence to enter into all mutually beneficial contracts and exchanges. Of course, such extremely high costs, if that is the price of accuracy, could deter the risk-averse litigant or the individual who has difficulty in funding an action. This latter point is a distributional problem that will be discussed in the next section.

In terms of efficiency, there are two issues. The first is to determine which type of system is the best. The second is to determine how to bring that system about. Current arrangements for reform in the judicial system involve a period of long, sometimes hesitant, but generally careful consideration followed by the imposition of any changes –

possibly after piloting and modification,[29] but with the expectation that the innovation will be applied uniformly and will last some time. Direct regulation of the system is what happens now, and it is certainly capable of delivering improvements on the *status quo*. Given the externality considerations explored above, it is clear that some public subsidy of the court system can be justified. The main challenge, then, is to devise ways that recognize the regulated (and subsidized) nature of the market while ensuring that transaction costs are kept low and product innovations are encouraged. Low user costs and allowing the consumer plentiful information and choice promise substantial dividends.

The Structure of Costs

One key parameter in this system is the matter of costs. In England and Wales excessive costs by opposing lawyers can be checked by vigorous use of wasted-costs orders, whereby legal representatives may be ordered to meet certain legal costs personally where that representative has been guilty of gross inefficiency or wilful obstruction. Such awards are currently very rare.[30] Costs themselves are already recognized in various modes:[31] standard basis (formerly known as *inter-partes* costs) and indemnity basis (formerly known as solicitor and client basis) or solicitor and own client basis (somewhat more generous, allowing all expenses reasonably incurred for the benefit of the client). More flexibility could be deployed with cost orders being imposed even on cases that settle at or before reaching the court-room door. All legal costs can currently be challenged and subjected to audit or taxation.

---

[29] The Middleton Report (1997, 4.14) backs the Law Society view that Woolf's reforms in civil procedure should be implemented in some regions ahead of others, thereby allowing some experimentation although with the aim of a uniform system in the end. In fact, all reform is to occur in a uniform manner. On the other hand, the Public Solicitor Defenders Office (PDSO) was introduced in Scotland in October 1998, initially on a pilot basis.

[30] See Zuckerman (1995), p. 172.

[31] See Zander (1996, p. 422) for more detail.

One suggestion by Middleton (1997, 2.44) is that not only should fixed price fees be agreed in advance but that these be filed with the court so that the award of costs when the case terminates would be based on the *lower* of the two figures. A set percentage of this would be paid by the client depending on the stage reached in proceedings, but any *inter-partes* costs would be computed on the basis of the lower of the fixed costs faced by the two parties. These practices could be incorporated in the efficiency norm for legal services.

Choice of Fee Structures

For consumers to be able to choose, there is a requirement for information regarding the service and its accompanying terms and conditions. Zuckerman (1995) draws on recommendations from the Australian Advisory Committee on Access to Justice to suggest that lawyers should ensure that clients have, not only details on the method by which the final bill will be computed, but also an estimate of the total costs that are likely and an estimate of the chances of success and the cost implications of failure. This information might also contain some details regarding alternative approaches to resolving the problem (in a non-litigious manner). We would go further and recommend (echoing Middleton) that there be an expectation that lawyers will be prepared to quote a fixed fee for handling the case (subject to insurance cover regarding the other side's costs, an increasingly common facility, discussed below). In this way, the risk of proceeding to litigation could be spread over many infrequent consumers of legal services – shifted, if one likes, from the inexperienced client to the lawyer who is in a better position to spread this risk.

Of course, these problems are currently not being faced to nearly the same extent by those (now relatively few) persons who qualify for full legal aid. The subsidized cost of legal services and the general immunity from the other side's costs in the event of failure results in a very different incentive structure when it comes to deciding whether or not to proceed to litigation. There is now a check made on a sample of all legal aid claims, although this process is

generally regarded as ineffective (Gray et al., 1996). More vigorous policing of such billings may well be introduced, although the intrinsic problem is not one of fraud but of the incentive structure that is built into the system with the state (or the other party) being left with most of the risk. The recent move to conditional fees and a system of tendering for legal aid contracts or franchises on the basis of fixed prices will mitigate this incentive problem (Middleton, 1997, 3.18 and the White Paper *Modernising Justice*, 1998, 2.42, 3.10).

Choice of Standard of Procedural Complexity

One other possible innovation from an efficiency point of view is to deregulate the system further by allowing the consumer to choose from competing standards of representation and procedural complexity (for example, rules of evidence and rules of discovery). Matters could be so arranged that the lowest cost alternative should dominate when the parties disagree, although subject to judicial oversight (Zuckerman, 1995). In this way agents would find the standard of justice that suits them best. The suggestion is that the system be made less monolithic, and that individuals be permitted to experiment and innovate by allowing more opportunity for direct expression of consumer choice. Competitive pressure can also be increased in the system, not simply by adjusting the volume of judicial services available but also by introducing innovative court-based procedures that are sensitive to consumer demands – for example, through the capping of legal expense to be incurred, or agreed limitations regarding the discovery and treatment of evidence (expert or other-wise), or to the design of the fee contract (between client and lawyer), and allowing the cost-shifting rule to be agreed between the parties. Lord Woolf's reforms have led to the establishment of certain pre-action protocols, for example in the use of expert witness(es).[32]

---

[32] *See Implementing Civil Reform – Progress Report.* Lord Chancellor's Department web site: http://www.open.gov.uk/lcd/civil/progrep2.htm.

This leaves the question of the positive externality to be addressed. Our previous argument suggests that cases which are likely to set a precedent and, hence, have a bearing on all subsequent cases of that type should be eligible for public funding. These have been identified as public interest cases by Middleton (1997, 5.17) who recommends a fourth track under the new English system with a special fund administered by the Legal Aid Board to cover their costs. A clear analogy can be drawn here with the readiness of the Law Commissioners of the Inland Revenue to bear both parties' costs in cases that are seen to be important in clarifying the interpretation of a piece of tax code.

Subsidy

There is also a case for some public funding of the civil courts because of the way in which the efficient disposition of cases reaching court allows individuals throughout the economy to avoid expensive pre-dispute contracting that would otherwise be necessary to protect their interests. Some commentators, such as Gravelle (1996), regard the prospect of determining when and where such public subsidy to be justified to be so complex that simply following market pricing at all stages of the process may, on balance, be the most effective approach. It is certainly true that market-responsive pricing would represent a marked improvement on the current administrative arrangements. The courts are well placed to take the lead. Judicial capacity could easily be made more responsive to market pressure. If pricing for access to court adjusts more flexibly to demand, in a way that reduces unwanted waiting time, then the entire system of dispute resolution will benefit from an increase in competition.

The judicial capacity of the system could be made more responsive to consumer demand by ensuring that court fees not only cover the running costs (including judicial salaries) but are allowed to lead directly to the appointment of additional judges as demand conditions reflect. While we argue above that ADR and the like provide a competitive

source of dispute resolution that tends to undermine any attempt by the formal system to exploit its monopoly power, that is because ADR and other mechanisms operate in the shadow of the law and, at the margin, compete with the judicial system for business.

Multi-Dimensional Approach

In general, the system should encourage innovation in technique and procedure. By increasing the freedom to experiment with rival systems of procedural arrangements – whether low-cost, abbreviated proceedings, or case management, or more inquisitorial-based procedures – then consumers would be able to choose, cafeteria-style, the level of justice that suits their needs, There is already evidence of change, but, to date, it has all come through a concerted effort with co-ordination across the whole judicial system. There is little room in the present system for experimentation or innovation. For example, the abolition of the notion of inferior courts with their restricted jurisdictions (for example, the Sheriff Courts in Scotland) would free parties to choose the venue in which to debate their cause.[33] Sheriffdoms having shorter queues or more attractive procedures would gain business to the detriment of those with a less attractive product range. Multiplicity of track – based on financial value of the cause in Woolf, and on legal complexity in Cullen – is a good idea that could compete in the market place of procedures alongside other innovations, preferably ones that provide consumers with choice.

---

[33] The current choice is between the relevant Sheriff Court and the Court of Session. As Lord Gill pointed out at The David Hume Institute conference, 'The Reform of Civil Justice', on 1 June 1998, this results in considerable congestion in the Court of Session with cases that would quite properly and appropriately be heard in the Sheriff Courts taking up the capacity of the Supreme Court.

V. Distributional Considerations

If, as suggested here, the state sector (courts) increases its reliance on market pricing as a way of determining the allocation of judicial resources, both towards tried and tested products (procedures) and for the more experimental specifications, there may well be an increase in the distributional problem because those with lower household income may not be able to afford to go to court. Of course many households cannot afford the luxury of a car. Some cannot even afford to take a bus. This does not generally call for market intervention.[34] But it is widely accepted that there is a communal interest in removing financial barriers to access to the courts. This argument is usually sustained by the view that access to justice should not be hindered by lack of means. There is also a general interest in having all valid grievances pursued irrespective of the economic circumstances of the litigant. Edward (1993, p. 13) argues:

> It is the litigant who identifies abuse of power and calls for it to be restrained. It is the litigant dissatisfied with the lame bureaucratic excuse who calls for a proper explanation. It is the litigant, refusing to lie down under political pressure or administrative highhandedness, who makes a nuisance of himself and goads his lawyer to action ...

That is true but it does not justify any cost – or at least not any cost to the public purse.

A valid reparation claim going unheard suggests an imperfection in the capital market or extreme risk aversion.

---

[34] The use of off-peak subsidized bus travel for senior citizens offers a counter-example.

An imperfect capital market becomes a problem when the injured party cannot sell the claim or borrow on the strength of the case to pursue the claim. Risk aversion arises when the party, possibly because of reduced personal circumstances, is not prepared to accept the risk of the litigation failing or disappointing. Both circumstances are likely with low-income households. The solution to date has been to provide legal aid. This ends up being expensive and exacerbates the supplier-induced demand problem that is present when any non-repeat buyer has to purchase legal services (Bowles, 1996). Policing mechanisms for the use and misuse of legal aid are not regarded as having been successful (Gray et al., 1996).

An alternative solution to legal aid is to allow conditional fee arrangements, whereby the risk and the capital outlay fall on the lawyer. For certain classes of grievance this seems to offer a viable solution and its use in all cases involving personal injury damages (excluding medical malpractice) in England and Wales, as was mentioned above, is currently emerging as the norm. But, for other types of dispute, what are often at stake are points of principle involving all-or-nothing outcomes where any pecuniary quantification of the issues is difficult, or inappropriate, and where financial compensation as mitigation is either not practicable (because of wealth constraints) or is not meaningful. Family law, and child custody in particular, are areas where such problems arise. In such situations, it is difficult to see how a person of modest means can enter into a gain-sharing arrangement with a lawyer.

One possible improvement would be to arrange the provision of state funds (through franchises) to be allocated in a contestable way over a variety of cases in a variety of jurisdictions and in a variety of classes of court-room. Performance could be judged by some weighting (politically determined) given to each type of case and allocated in much the same way as public spending across various medical services is allocated in certain states in the USA (Dingwall et al., 1997; Williams, 1995). If such a weighting

system of public fund allocation is adopted, it would be important to include in the payment mechanism used to reward the agency responsible (the Legal Aid Board or the Community Legal Services Agency) a measure of disputes not reaching the formal stage of a summons being issued but resolved privately. These are as much a part of the service delivery of the civil justice system as the cases that reach the courts.

One problem that arises is if the maximization of the performance criteria *per se* leads to behaviour that is not wholly consistent with the maximization of the true objective – the delivery of a quality service. This is likely to occur when the defined performance targets are not adequately drawn up. This dysfunctional impact of non-market incentive systems was a common problem in centrally planned economies (where the plan might suggest a production target of one million washers but omit to specify the diameter, thickness or some other vital aspect, leading to the production of the least-cost version that complies with the plan).

Allowing the choice of venue to be contestable would add an element of competition on the supply side. Benchmark competition could also be introduced by the provision of state-employed solicitors (along the lines of the Edinburgh pilot scheme of the Public Defenders Solicitors Office for criminal defence in Scotland). The absence of consumer choice of lawyer in such arrangements has been answered by Lord Hardie (1997, p. 483) in terms of expecting to be able to choose the roofer when he hires someone to fix his roof, but not expecting to have a say in the selection of the pilot when one flies down to London. But it is worth remembering, in the context of publicly employed solicitors, that in trying to repair one market imperfection, another may be introduced – here in the form of potential loss of efficiency when the market is set aside.

For the middle classes who are among the most vociferous critics regarding their restricted access to justice, the simple fact will remain: you pay your money and you

take your choice. Encouraging reform of the system to become a more cafeteria-style of arrangement, by enlarging that choice and possibly putting downward pressure on the money needed to have one's day in court, may extend some more palatable modes of dispute resolution, even to the middle classes.

VI. Conclusions

Reform in England and Wales currently seems to be developing a head of steam (Middleton, 1997; White Paper *Modernising Justice*, 1998). In Scotland the recent reforms in the Sheriff Courts (Morris and Headrick, 1995; Samuel and Bell, 1997) reassure us that the idea of reform is far from a novelty. In terms of dispute resolution, the state sector, in the guise of the civil justice system, influences the way negotiations are carried out and ensures agreements are enforced (diligence). But it is also a major source of dispute resolution in its own right, and in this way it exerts a major influence on dispute resolution and individual behaviour throughout the whole economy. Increased competitiveness in the state sector will invigorate the entire system of dispute resolution, to the benefit of all and not just for those who go to court.

There are in circulation many good ideas regarding procedural reform in the civil justice system. These include fast-track procedures, judicial case management, conditional fees, contingent fees, franchising of legal aid, and so on. Rather than striving *ex ante* to find the optimum combination of these possibilities and imposing it on the entire system of civil justice, one possibility would be to introduce a market-led expansion of judicial capacity by allowing court fees to be determined by market forces with the proceeds ploughed back into judicial capacity. This would offer more competition for the alternative dispute-resolution industry and be to the benefit of consumers of dispute-resolution services (both of the formal court-based variety and ADR). Given that the object of the system of civil justice is to further the interests of those who pay for it – whether directly by fees or indirectly through the tax system – one is bound to ask whether the safeguards in place in the

existing system offer the most effective way of furthering that end.

A reasonable defence might be offered for the view that the suppliers of the judicial services are so constrained by professional ethics, by law, and by associated regulations, that clients are indeed well served. That defence might be elaborated as follows: (i) solicitors and advocates/barristers are bound by professional standards enforced by their professional associations to advise clients whether or not to proceed with or to defend an action and to reveal if there are circumstances which prevent them taking on a case, such as a conflict of interest or doubts about the identity of the principal of whom the lawyer is the agent; (ii) lawyers, following client care rules, are enjoined to clarify how their charges are computed and to warn clients that the final bill is beyond their control because of uncertainties surrounding the time scale, the complexity and the outcome of the action; and (iii) comprehensive procedures are in place in order to deal with complaints by clients about the service offered by lawyers.

Whatever the merits of this defence of the *status quo*, the individual client not continually engaged in litigation is in an exposed position.[35] The nature of the product, justice, is elusive and is naturally defined by the client as a judgement in his or her favour, an outcome which cannot be guaranteed whatever the cost incurred. For many consumers, assessment of the chances of success in an action cannot be based on experience derived from regular purchase of the service, but rests on the quality of the advice of the lawyer who, unless his services are in excessive demand, has an interest in going to law on the client's behalf. A lawyer cannot give a precise estimate of the cost of proceeding with or defending a case, except to explain how charges are made up, but he or she can benefit materially from the length and complexity of an action. These factors

---

[35] A casual reading of McCormack's *The Terrible Truth about Lawyers* (1987) brings this home quite clearly.

may reflect the desire to maintain the quality of justice, but it is the client who pays for this and not the lawyers, unless it is agreed to share these costs as with a no-win no-fee system.

While a comprehensive complaints system may act as a deterrent to professional negligence and malpractice, it can only operate retrospectively, which is of little use to an individual client who has needlessly lost a case and who has to incur the time and expense involved in pursuing a complaint. In any case, the Legal Ombudsmen for Scotland and for England and Wales have no means at their disposal to obtain redress for clients, to discipline or fine lawyers along the lines available to the regulators of the personal pensions system.

In short, the client is, as we have already suggested, in a similar position to those obliged to accept cost-plus contracts once they are locked onto a transaction in which the outcome is far from certain. Their defences against exploitation suggest an agenda for making the judicial system more responsive to individual needs.

First, as in defence contracting, some form of competitive tendering is desirable, offering an incentive for suppliers of legal services to give the fullest information on the nature of the service provided. Informative advertising should be the rule rather than the exception. Voluntary organizations supporting ordinary citizens, such as the Citizens' Advice Bureaux should press professional legal bodies for the fullest description of lawyers' services and obligations. One step forward would be to break down the process of seeking redress in law into two parts, whereby advice as to what is needed or what is possible could be obtained from one source, while prescription could be filled by another source, possibly after some shopping around. The advice network proposed in *Access to Justice. Beyond the Year 2000* may be a step in this direction. There will be difficulties, however, as the nature of the remedy is so tightly bound to the delivery of the remedy. Persuading one practitioner to accept blindly and follow the prescription of another practitioner

would threaten professional values. But franchising and competitive tendering for legal aid contracts may eventually make this approach more generally acceptable.

Second, and as a possible adjunct to the above approach, clients should be informed of the alternative ways in which they can pursue or defend an action, including seeking agreement on whether to go for the fast-track method, ADR, or follow the conventional routes. Information about alternative sources of the supply of justice, with the prospects that quality has to be traded off against cost, should be a clearly recognized professional responsibility. Alternative procedural arrangements and fee contracts should be investigated, and product innovation encouraged.

Third, the client must be assured that the discretionary element introduced into the costs that he must bear as a result of entering the judicial process are minimized, if not eliminated. This reinforces the view that the cardinal element in his protection is efficient management of the process. This could involve giving power to trial judges to control the passage of a case from the time it is raised until it is decided (case management). In other words, the task can only be assigned to those who have no financial interest in the judicial process involved in the case. How this is to be achieved is a sensitive matter because it entails a radical change in the existing system.

Fourth, the supply of judges must be addressed. The supply of judicial inputs should be made more responsive to market signals. Charging court fees to reflect full costs is a start in this direction. The logical step after that is to initiate additional judicial appointments where market projections suggest they can be self-sustaining in revenue terms. The positive externality aspect of civil justice can be addressed by subsidizing identified public interest cases as has been suggested in the context of legal aid reform, or by subsidizing court proceedings in general (and particularly at the appeal stage). The problem is as old as Adam Smith (1776), who puzzled over the question of how to offer incentives to judges to dispense justice efficiently. Interestingly enough, he considered that judges should be

paid per case and should be paid only when the case was completed!

Such is the case of the advocates of reform, following the principle of maximizing benefits to the consumers of justice. If the principle is accepted, but the suggested reforms are not, then the onus of proof lies with critics to show why they should be rejected and/or how they might be improved. Not to accept the principle, however, risks leaving the legal profession open to the charge that the system of civil justice is a *Ding an sich* designed primarily to promote its own interests.

Glossary

Advocate: in Scotland this job title is equivalent to barrister in England and Wales and trial-lawyer in the USA. It, as the title suggests, is a lawyer who specializes in pleading or arguing a case (usually in court). Advocates no longer have the sole right of audience in the Court of Session as solicitor-advocates may now appear.

Bar Council: the professional body that regulates the profession of barrister, that is those who specialize in trial procedure and, until 1995, had the sole right of audience in the Crown Court and the High Court in England and Wales.

Champerty: where a third party funds litigation in an understanding that they will receive part of the damages recovered by the plaintiff if the case is successful. Occasionally this concept is grouped with barratry and maintenance (Painter, 1995). Traditionally forbidden in England and Wales, the common law offence was abolished in the Criminal Law Act 1967, and in 1995 the Lord Chancellor, under the provisions of the Courts and Legal Services Act 1990, explicitly permitted conditional fees which allow the lawyer and client to agree on a fee-plus-uplift if successful and no-fee if unsuccessful (as opposed to contingent fees where a given percentage of the damages goes to the plaintiff's legal team in lieu of fees). The uplift could be up to 100 per cent of the normal hourly based fee, where lower uplifts would be appropriate when the probability of success was higher.

Circuit Judge: a judge (part-time) in the Crown Court (criminal) system in England and Wales who has served at least three years as a Recorder.

Civil justice: that part of the legal system that is available to individuals who wish to seek redress or compensation for some wrong done to them. It includes matters relating to contracts, personal injury and family matters. It should be contrasted with the criminal justice system which, almost always, concerns the behaviour of the state as it seeks to punish and hence deter wrong-doing.

Court of Session: the senior court for civil procedures in Scotland. It is a court of first instance (the Outer House) with a jurisdiction that substantially overlaps that of the Sheriff Courts. It hears appeals from the Sheriff Courts, can hear own appeals (in the Inner House) and a case can be appealed to the House of Lords.

Diligence: the enforcement of any court ruling obtained against a defender.

Discovery provisions: the entitlements available to each party in terms of examining the evidence available to the other side in advance of a court-room appearance. This is essentially integrated into the Scottish system of written pleadings where the arguments and rebuttals that comprise the kernel of the case must be carefully laid out to the agreement of both sides.

District Judge: judge in the County Court (civil) system in England and Wales. Formerly (until 1990) known as county court registrars.

Faculty of Advocates: the professional body that regulates the conduct of advocates in the Scottish courts (cf. the Bar Council in England and Wales for barristers).

High Court: in England and Wales, the most senior court of first instance. In criminal procedure it ranks above the Crown Courts (which are themselves superior to the Magistrates Courts). In civil procedure the High Court

ranks above the County Courts which are senior to the Magistrates Courts. In Scotland, the High Court is the superior court of criminal jurisdiction (sitting above the Sheriff Courts and the district courts). Only criminal proceedings are heard in the High Court in Scotland (the Court of Session being the equivalent civil procedure court).

Inter-partes costs: the category of costs that are allowed, subject to the scrutiny of the Taxing Master in England and Wales or the Auditor of the Court in Scotland, when the losing side is required to pay the other party's costs (as is generally the case under the English rule). This is a less generous or less all-encompassing basis than solicitor-and-own-client costs. See Hurst (1995).

Loser-pays: sometimes known as the English rule but, in truth, the approach adopted in most jurisdictions outside North America, whereby the losing party is responsible for paying the legal fees and expenses of the prevailing party. This contrasts with the American rule where, in general, each side pays its own costs irrespective of the outcome.

Proof: trial in a civil case before a judge sitting without a jury in the Scottish system.

Queen's Counsel: in England and Wales, the senior level of barrister appointed, on consultation, by the Lord Chancellor. The term silk is sometimes used in a reference to the style of gown worn. This elevation usually means a higher fee can be commanded. A roughly similar system applies for advocates in Scotland.

Recorders: judges (part-time) in the Crown Court (criminal) system in England and Wales and appointed for a limited period.

Reparation: the area of Scots law, sometimes known as delict and similar to tort in the English system, where one

individual seeks compensation, or some other remedy, from another party for an infringement of his/her legal rights by that other party.

Sheriff Courts: courts in Scotland that hear both civil and criminal cases over a wide range of gravity and importance. Jurisdiction of each court is restricted to that of a particular sheriffdom (there are forty-nine Sheriff Courts organized into six sheriffdoms). Very minor criminal cases are more likely to go to the District Courts, particularly serious criminal cases to the High Court, and particularly complex civil cases to the Court of Session. The senior judge in each of the six sheriffdoms known as Sheriff Principal and the other judges, each assigned to a particular sheriffdom, are known as sheriffs.

Summary Cause: in the Sheriff Courts this applies to a case where the value of the cause does not exceed £1,500 – usually related to recovery of debts or possessions. Somewhat relaxed procedural rules apply regarding, for example, the recording of evidence given.

Taxed costs: when, under the system of cost allocation that is generally used in Europe, the losing side is ordered to pay the costs (expenses in Scotland) of the successful party in a civil litigation, the costs that must be so paid are subject to the scrutiny of the court. This is done by a Taxing Master in England and Wales and by the Auditor of Court in Scotland. The costs so awarded are usually *inter-partes* costs (see above).

Tort: the part of the common law that relates to civil justice. The area is known as delict in Scotland. Common law is the body of law that is judge-made, in the sense that it rests on previous cases and the judgements therein. It can be contrasted with public law which generally concerns various laws passed by Parliament.

References

Baldwin, Robert (1997) *Regulating legal services*. London: Lord Chancellor's Department Research Series no. 5/97.

Baumol, William (1996) 'Children of Performing Arts, the Economic Dilemma', *Journal of Cultural Economics*, (20 October) pp. 183–206.

Benson, Bruce L. (1997) 'Jurisdiction: Privatization of legal and administrative services', in Herbert Giersch (ed.), *Merits and Limits of Markets*. Berlin: Springer, pp. 111–139.

Bernstein, Lisa (1992) 'Opting out of the legal system: extralegal contractual relations in the diamond industry', *Journal of Legal Studies*, vol. 21, pp. 115–157.

Bevan, Gwyn (1996) 'Has there been supplier-induced demand for legal aid?' *Civil Justice Quarterly*, vol. 15, pp. 58–114.

Bowles, Roger (1996) 'Reform of legal aid and the solicitor's profession', *Hume Papers on Public Policy*, vol. 4, no. 4, pp. 4–23.

Cullen, W. Douglas, Lord (1995) *Review of the business of the Outer House of the Court of Session*. Edinburgh: Scottish Courts Administration.

Dingwall, Robert, Fenn, Paul, and Truck, Jackie (1997) *Rationing and cost-containment in legal services*. London: A report to the Lord Chancellor's Department (July).

Domberg, Simon, and Sherr, Avrom (1995) 'The impact of competition on pricing and quality of legal services', in Matthew Bishop, John Kay and Colin Mayer (eds) *The Regulatory Challenge*. Oxford: Oxford University Press, pp. 119–137.

Doriat, Myriam, and Deffains, Bruno (1998) 'The dynamics of pre-trial negotiation in France: is there a deadline effect in the French legal system?'. Paper presented to the European Law and Economics Association. Utrecht (September).

Edward, David A.O. (1993) *The Role of Law in the Rule of Law*. Presidential Address to The David Hume Institute. Edinburgh: Hume Occasional Paper, no. 42.

Fiss, Owen (1984) 'Against settlement', *Yale Law Review*, vol. 93, no. 6 (May), pp. 1073–1090.

Friedman, David (1979) 'Private creation and enforcement of law: a historic case', *Journal of Legal Studies*, vol. 8, pp. 399–415.

Galanter, Marc (1983) 'Reading the landscape of disputes: what we know and don't know (and think we know) about our allegedly contentious and litigious society', UCLA Law Review, vol. 31, no. 1 (October), pp. 4–71.

Genn, Hazel (1987) *Hard Bargaining: Out of Court Settlement in Personal Injury Actions*. Oxford: Oxford University Press.

Gill, Lord (1997) 'The Woolf, Cullen and Coulon reports', *Journal of the Law Society of Scotland*, vol. 42, no. 11, pp. 437–439.

Goriely, Tamara (1997) *Contracting for Civil Litigation: Modelling Volumes, Access and Regional Distributions for Certificated Non-Matrimonial Civil Legal Aid*. Prepared for the Lord Chancellor's Department (September). TPR Social & Legal Research: London.

Goriely, Tamara, and Paterson, Alan A. (1996) 'Provision and access to legal services: a European comparison'. Paper prepared for the Scottish Home and Health Department and Law Society of England and Wales.

Gravelle, Hugh (1996) 'What price should be charged for civil justice?', *Hume Papers on Public Policy*, vol. 4, no. 4, pp. 36–52.

Gray, Alistair, Fenn, Paul, and Rickman, Neil (1996) 'Monitoring legal aid: Back to first principles?', *Hume Papers on Public Policy*, vol. 4, no. 4, pp. 24–35.

Hardie, Lord (1997) 'Funding justice in Scotland', *Journal of the Law Society of Scotland Journal*, vol. 42, no. 12, pp. 480–484.

Hume, David (1777) 'My own life', in Eugene Millar (ed.) *David Hume: Essays Moral, Political, and Literary.* Indianapolis: Liberty Fund (1985), pp. xxxi–xli.

Hurst, Peter T. (1995) *Civil Costs*. London: Sweet & Maxwell.

Landes, William M., and Posner, Richard A. (1979) 'Adjudication as a private good', *Journal of Legal Studies*, vol. 8, pp. 235–284.

Lord Chancellor's Department (1998) *Modernising Justice. The Government's Plans for Reforming Legal Services and the Courts.* White Paper, Cmnd. 4155.

McCormack, Mark H. (1987) *The Terrible Truth about Lawyers.* London: William Collins Sons & Co.

McCutcheon, John (1998) 'The profitability of legal practices in Scotland'. Journal of the Law Society of Scotland, vol. 43, no. 3, pp. 90–94.

Main, Brian G. M. (1997) 'An economic perspective on the costs of justice', *Hume Papers on Public Policy*, vol. 5, no. 4, pp. 1–28.

Middleton, Sir Peter (1997) *Review of Civil Justice and Legal Aid. Report to the Lord Chancellor by Sir Peter Middleton GCB.* London: Lord Chancellor's Department (September).

Miller, Ann, and Morris, Sue (1994) 'Legal services in Scotland: consumer survey', *Legal Studies Research Findings* No. 1. Edinburgh: The Scottish Office Central Research Unit.

Mnookin, Robert H., and Kornhauser, Lewis (1979) 'Bargaining in the shadow of the law: the case of divorce', *The Yale Law Journal*, vol. 88, no. 5 (April), pp. 950–997.

Morris, Sue, and Headrick, Debbie (1995) *Pilgrim's Process? Defended Actions in the Sheriff's Ordinary Court.* Edinburgh: The Scottish Office Central Research Unit.

Murray, Andrew (1997) 'Fair notice – the role of written pleadings in the Scottish justice system', *Hume Papers on Public Policy*, vol. 5, no. 4, pp. 49–65.

Ogus, Anthony (1997) 'Civil procedure reform and economic analysis', University of Manchester, Law School, Working Paper.

Ogus, Anthony (1999) 'Lawyers as designers or disputants? Some observations of the economics of civil justice'. *Hume Papers on Public Policy*, vol. 7, no. 1 pp. 28–36.

Painter, Richard W. (1995) 'Litigating on a contingency: a monopoly of champions or a market for champerty?' *Chicago-Kent Law Review*, vol. 71, no. 2 – Symposium on Fee Shifting.

Peacock, Alan (1994) 'The costs of justice: an economist's approach', in *The Costs of Justice*, Hume Occasional Paper, The David Hume Institute, pp. 18–30.

Peacock, Alan (1998) 'Cost of judicial services' *The New Palgrave Dictionary of Economics and the Law*, vol. 1, pp. 530–536.

Reeves, Peter (1998) *Silk Cut: Are Queen's Counsel Necessary?* London: Adam Smith Institute.

Rickman, Neil, and Fenn, Paul (1998) 'Insuring litigation risk: some recent developments in England and Wales', *The Geneva Papers on Risk and Insurance*, vol. 23, no. 87 (April), pp. 210–223.

Rosen, Sherwin (1981) 'The economics of superstars', *American Economic Review*, vol. 71, no. 5, pp. 845–858.

Rosen, Sherwin (1992) 'The market for lawyers', *Journal of Law and Economics*, vol. 35 (October), pp. 215–246.

Samuel, Elaine, and Bell, Robert (1997) *Defended Ordinary Actions in the Sheriff Court: Implementing O.C.R. (93)*. Edinburgh: The Scottish Office Home Department, Central Research Unit.

Scottish Court Service (1997) *Annual Report and Accounts 1996–97*. Edinburgh: The Stationery Office.

Scottish Office (1998) *Access to Justice. Beyond the Year 2000*. Edinburgh: Department of Home and Health.

Smith, Adam (1776) *An Inquiry into the Nature and Causes of the Wealth of Nations*, edited by R. H. Campbell and A.S. Skinner. Oxford: Clarendon Press, 1996, pp. 708–723.

Stephen, Frank, and Love, James H. (1996) 'Deregulation of legal services markets in the UK: evidence from conveyancing', *Hume Papers on Public Policy*, vol. 4, no. 4
pp. 53–66.

Stephen, Frank, and Love, James H. (1999) 'Regulation of the legal profession: A survey of the theoretical and empirical literature', in B. Boukaerts and G. DeGeest (eds.,) *Encyclopaedia of Law and Economics*, Edward Elgar.

Tan, Y. L. (1990) 'Champertous contracts and assignments', *Quarterly Law Review*, vol. 106 (October) pp. 656–679.

Wadia, Rachel (1997) 'Judicial case management. The quiet but significant revolution', *Hume Papers on Public Policy*, vol. 5, no. 4, pp. 66–95.

Walker, David M. (1997) *The Scottish Legal System. An introduction to the study of Scots Law*. Edinburgh: W. Green/Sweet & Maxwell, 7th Edition.

Williams, Alan (1995) 'Similarities between health care system and criminal justice system', notes prepared for a presentation to the Lord Chancellor's Economists' Conference. London (April).

Woolf, The Right Honourable, Lord (1995) *Access to Justice. Interim Report.* London: HMSO (June).

Woolf, The Right Honourable, Lord (1996) *Access to Justice. Final Report.* London: HMSO (July).

Yarrow, Stella (1998) *The Price of Success. Lawyers, Clients and Conditional Fees.* London: Policy Studies Institute for the Lord Chancellor's Advisory Committee on Legal Education and Conduct.

Zander, Michael (1995) 'Why Lord Woolf's proposed reforms of civil litigation should be rejected', in *Reform of Civil Procedure. Essays on Access to Justice*, edited by A. A. S. Zuckerman and Ross Cranston. Oxford: Clarendon Press, pp. 79–95.

Zander, Michael (1996) *Cases and Materials on the English Legal System.* London: Butterworths (7th Edition).

Zuckerman, A. A. S. (1995) 'A Reform of civil procedure – rationing procedure rather than access to justice', *Journal of Law and Society*, vol. 22, no. 2 (June), pp. 155–188.

Zuckerman, A. A. S. (1996) 'Lord Woolf's Access to Justice: Plus ça change…' *Modern Law Review*, vol. 59, pp. 773.

COMMENTARY:

Interjurisdictional Competition Through Alternative Dispute Resolution: A Commentary on *What Price Civil Justice?*[1]

Bruce L. Benson

[1] I want to thank Colin Robinson for asking me to provide this commentary on *What Price Civil Justice?*, and Brian Main and Sir Alan Peacock for allowing my remarks to accompany their excellent paper. Various passages and sections of the following presentation are drawn from published or forthcoming writings (see Benson, 1998a, 1998b, 1999b, 2000a, 2000c, 2000d).

I. Introduction

Brian Main and Sir Alan Peacock's detailed exploration of the determinants of the price of civil justice in England and Wales and Scotland, and of potential reforms to lower that price, is generally right on target. This commentary simply elaborates on the benefits of introducing more competition into the legal system by exploring one of their proposals in more detail: the use of alternative dispute resolution (ADR). In order to do so, three intertwined and commonly held but flawed beliefs about ADR are discussed. Specifically, the view that ADR mechanisms are simply procedural options is addressed in section II where it is explained that ADR can actually provide a mechanism for choosing an alternative set of substantive rules. That is, ADR can enhance competition by facilitating the choice of among legal jurisdictions. The belief that ADR cannot be a source of precedent is examined in Section III, where it is explained that ADR can also produce substantive rules. Section IV dispenses with the contention that a formal court system backed by the coercive power of government is a necessary prerequisite for effective ADR. Privately produced sanctions can back privately produced dispute resolution and induce parties to recognize the substantive rules of a non-state legal jurisdiction. Section V concludes by emphasizing some of the benefits of interjurisdictional competition through the use of ADR.

II. ADR as a Mechanism for Jurisdictional Choice[2]

ADR is often characterized exclusively as a procedural option for resolution of disputes. Procedural benefits include the facts that: (1) mediators or arbitrators can be selected for their expertise in matters pertinent to a dispute, thus reducing the potential for judicial error as well as the time costs of and expenditures on dispute–resolution relative to litigation; (2) as less adversarial procedures than litigation, both mediation and arbitration are more likely to sustain repeated-dealing relationships; (3) if desired, privacy can be maintained; and (4) mediation and arbitration services can be purchased in a market without the costly delay that arises when court time is allocated by waiting. But ADR may also be an attractive jurisdictional option.

The argument that ADR provides a mechanism for jurisdictional choice can be seen most easily by considering the customary commercial law which is the primary source of order in international trade (Berman and Dasser, 1990; Benson, 1992a, 1999b, 2000a, 2000c, 2000d; Draetta et al., 1992). Almost all international trade contracts have clauses that expressly exclude adjudication by the national courts of the trading parties and refer any dispute that cannot be resolved through negotiation or mediation to arbitration (Berman and Dasser, 1990: p. 33; Casella, 1992: p. 1). Not surprisingly, given this reliance on arbitration clauses as the mechanism for avoiding national jurisdictions, there are many potential sources of arbitration for international business disputes. A large number of international trade associations have their own conflict–resolution procedures, using arbitrators with special expertise in trade matters of concern to association members (over three decades ago, for

---

[2] This section is drawn from Benson (1998a, 1999b).

example, Lazarus, et al., 1965 discussed more than 120 such tribunals). Other traders rely on the International Chamber of Commerce (ICC) and its arbitration institution. ICC arbitrators are experts in international commerce, and are typically chosen from a different national origin from those of the parties in the dispute. International arbitration procedures are speedy and flexible, in reflection of commercial interest. Arbitrators from the American Arbitration Association (AAA) and similar groups from other countries may also be employed.

A contract can also specify the substantive law and conflict-of-law rules under which any dispute should be resolved, perhaps by designating the contract law of the seat of arbitration or of some other national legal system. The 'usual way' of determining the relevant substantive law for international commercial arbitration, however, is to decide cases 'exclusively on the interpretation of contracts and the relevance of trade usages so that very little depends on the question of the applicable [national] law' (Böckstiegal, 1984, pp. 27, 23). Lew's (1978, p. 581) detailed analysis of available records (also see Trakman, 1983 and Draetta et al., 1992) reveals that in principle, 'The answer to every dispute is to be found *prima facie* in the contract itself. What did the parties intend, what did they agree and what did they expect?' When an arbitrator cannot discover the parties' intent in the contract, however, the focus turns to consideration of what the parties expected or should have expected, and in this regard, international arbitrators generally intentionally 'denationalize' their awards, making them acceptable by showing their consistency with accepted traditional practices and usage (customary rules) which are commonly recognized within the 'private international law systems from which the parties come' (Lew, 1978, pp. 582–585).

In international trade at least, it is easy to see that the choice of arbitration over litigation is often a jurisdictional choice, but commercial contracts, business custom and/or other rules determined within commercial organizations are

also the sources of 'law' that commercial arbitrators consider within many domestic commercial organisations too (Benson, 1995, 1999b). For instance, consider Bernstein's (1992) description of the rejection of state-made law through the use of mediation and arbitration by the diamond merchant community. Furthermore, while the role of private dispute resolution as a means of applying customary norms is more difficult to recognize outside the commercial area because the ADR tends to be less formal (indeed, in some cases the processes are 'illegal' under the state's law – see de Soto, 1989 and Benson, 1998d, pp. 94–126 for instance) and because the explicit contractual agreement to use ADR is often not present, the fact is that such arrangements tend to be very important.[3] Numerous examples of centralized coercive systems can be cited where 'parallel' predominately co-operative systems of norms and institutions actually dominate many and at times even most

---

[3] Formal ADR can also be used to resolve disputes outside organized business communities, however, as evidenced by the long-term success of the New York Stock Exchange's arbitration of disputes between members and their customers (Lazarus, et al., 1965, p. 27). A number of other formal ADR arrangements also exist to deal with disputes between businesses and their customers, between neighbours, between groups dealing with environmental disputes, and so on (Benson, 1990, pp. 213–224). Grievance arbitration between labourers and employees is also widespread (see Benson, 2000a for discussion). In fact, the use of a formal ADR process does not require a pre-existing contractual agreement. For instance, in the United States, entrepreneurs began to recognize an opportunity in the late 1970s and early 1980s to offer formal processes of dispute resolution to anyone who might want to avoid the crowded and expensive public court system, and private for-profit firms began entering the market. They now resolve a wide variety of disputes, including personal injury disputes, divorces, construction warranty disputes, disputes over loan defaults, and so on. The industry has continued to grow and competition is increasing. More than fifty private-for-profit dispute-resolution firms were operating in the US in 1992, reflecting the 'demand for relief from the jammed dockets and killer jury awards of the courts' (Phalon, 1992, p. 126). See Benson (1998d, pp. 115–116) for more discussion.

interactions even outside 'legally' recognized groups like trade associations (de Soto, 1989; Ellickson, 1991; Benson, 1998d). Indeed, the historical importance of state-made and enforced rules as actual determinants of behaviour is probably much less than is popularly perceived, since people rely on norms (including customs, conventions, etc.) to govern much of their behaviour even when some formal rule of law may appear to apply (de Soto, 1989; Ellickson, 1991). Customary rules probably are the primary source of 'social order' (Fuller, 1981; Ellickson, 1991; Benson, 1989, 1998b, 1998c, 2000b).

III. ADR as a Source of Precedent in Customary Law[4]

A 'customary law' is an obligation that is widely recognized and accepted by the individuals in the affected group. The original source of widely accepted customs are often not known, but in all likelihood, they started as conventions, contractual promises, or means of resolving disputes for some individuals and then spread through the relevant community. Indeed, a key distinguishing characteristic of a customary rule is that it is initiated by an individual's decision to behave in particular ways under particular circumstances. Adopting a behavioural pattern creates expectations on the part of others and accompanying obligations (Hayek, 1973, pp. 96–97). Then, as numerous individuals who interact with one another observe each others' behavioural patterns, emulating those that appear desirable, such behaviour and obligations spread (Mises, 1957, p. 192). In other words, customary rules evolve spontaneously from the bottom up rather than being intentionally designed by a legislator or a judge, and they are voluntarily accepted rather than being imposed, even though no explicit statement declares their relevance. The result is analogous to a unanimity (or consensus) rule for collective decision-making. If some individuals choose not to adopt all of the rules, they will not be members of that customary community.

A unanimity requirement implies that a rule of obligation is not going to be adopted if some individuals expect that the rule will be biased against them, that it will fail to support decisions that enhance their chances for wealth production, or that it will generate greater personal costs

---

[4] Much of this section is drawn from Benson (2000a). Additional elaboration appears in Benson (1999b).

than personal benefits. Indeed, customary law tends to be quite conservative in the sense that it guards against mistakes. However, customary law can change quite rapidly when conditions warrant it.

If a set of individuals decide that, for their purposes, behaviour that was attractive in the past has ceased to be useful, they can voluntarily devise a new contract stipulating any behaviour that they wish. Through negotiation and contracting, existing custom can be quickly replaced by a new rule of obligation towards certain other individuals without prior consent of or simultaneous recognition by everyone in the group. Individuals entering into contracts with these parties are informed of the contractual innovation, and/or others outside the contract observe the results of a new contractual stipulation, so if it provides a more desirable behaviour rule than older custom, it can be rapidly emulated. Many contracts spread quickly as 'standard forms' throughout the relevant community (Rubin, 1995, p. 115). Contracting may actually be the most important source of new rules in a dynamic system of customary law (Fuller, 1981. p. 157). For example, many innovations in commercial law have been initiated in contracts before quickly spreading through the relevant merchant community (Berman 1983, pp. 349–355; Benson 1989, 1998b, 1998c; Draetta et al. 1992).

Alternatively, the inadequacy of existing customary rules can be revealed when a dispute arises. Negotiation is probably the primary means of dispute resolution for members of a close-knit customary law community, reinforcing the contention that contracting is a primary mechanism for initiating rapid change in customary law. If direct negotiation fails, however, the parties to a dispute within a customary enterprise of law often turn to a third party for assistance. ADR in the form of mediation or arbitration can then clarify existing rules and create new rules if none clearly apply. This is definitely the case within modern international commercial communities (Lew, 1978; Benson, 1989, 1992a, 1998b), for instance, as well as for many domestic

commercial communities (Bernstein, 1992; Benson, 1995). Since a dispute suggests that existing rules are unclear or insufficient, new customary rules can be and often are initiated as mediators or arbitrators resolve the disputes (Fuller, 1981, p. 90, 110–111; Lew, 1978, pp. 584–589; Benson, 1989, 1998b, 1998c, 2000b). Unlike public court precedent, such dispute resolutions only apply to the parties in the dispute, of course, but if the resolution suggests a rule that appears to be more effective at facilitating interactions than previously existing customary rules have been, the rule can spread rapidly through the community.

This contention that ADR can be a source of precedent is frequently denied. For instance, Brunet (1987, p.19) contends that 'the output of conventional litigation should be viewed as a public good – society gains more from litigation than would be produced if litigation were left to the private market'. This presumably is the case because the results of arbitration and other forms of ADR are 'internal' to the parties involved (Brunet, 1987, pp. 14–15) so they will either not produce precedent, or will under produce precedent. Similarly, Landes and Posner (1979, pp. 238, 239, 245) argue that 'because of the difficulty of establishing property rights in a precedent, private ... judges might deliberately avoid explaining their results because the demand for their services would be reduced by rules that, by clarifying the meaning of the law, reduce the incidence of disputes'; that 'a problem is that a system of voluntary adjudication is strongly biased against the creation of precise rules of any sort'; and further, that commercial arbitration is 'not a source of rules or precedents'. One reason for such arguments is that secrecy is often a characteristic of arbitration. For instance, Bernstein (1992, p. 124) explains that within the diamond industry 'As long as judgments are complied with, the fact of the arbitration as well as its outcome are officially kept secret'. But this 'official' secrecy does not mean that precedents are never created, or that too few rules exist. The parties to the dispute will certainly consider the arbitration result in future dealings under similar circumstances, for

instance, and probably have to explain them to trading partners. But more importantly, a diamond bourse (trading club) is an information exchange as much as it is a commodities exchange. As one author put it, 'the bourse grapevine is the best in the world. It has been going for years and moves with the efficiency of a satellite communications network. ... Bourses are the fountainhead of this information and from them it is passed out along the tentacles that stretch around the world' as each local bourse is part of an umbrella organization that, among other things, arbitrates disputes between members of different bourses, enforces arbitration judgments from other bourses, and facilitates the establishment of uniform trading rules throughout the industry (Bernstein, 1992, p. 121). Under such a circumstance, 'official' secrecy is probably not much of a constraint on the spread of important information about an arbitration ruling that might provide new precedent. It is clear that in the diamond industry arbitration results do 'become known through gossip' (Bernstein, 1992, p. 126) at any rate.

Bernstein (1992, pp. 126–127) contends that when diamond industry arbitrators hear complex cases 'it is difficult to determine what substantive rules of decisions are applied', and such observations may appear in support of the view that arbitration does not produce effective precedent. However, as Fuller (1981, p. 90) explains, 'Even if there is no statement by the tribunal of the reasons for its decision, some reason will be perceived or guessed at, and the parties will tend to govern their conduct accordingly'. Thus, precedent of a sort may well be produced even in such an environment. Furthermore, and importantly, it must be recognized that within a customary legal system there are a number of ways for new rules to evolve (for example, through unilateral adoption of behaviour that is observed and emulated, through bilateral negotiation or mediation and contracting with resulting contract clauses spreading and becoming standardised), besides through precedent (Benson, 1998b), so when a particular arbitration process

does not appear to be designed to produce precedent it simply may mean that precedent is a relatively unimportant source of new rules for the relevant group, or that circumstances do not change often enough to require new rules. And importantly, if situations change, making precedent more important, the group is also free to change its arbitration procedures. Thus, as Bernstein (1992, p. 150) explains, diamond dealers have begun to recognize that 'The lack of written decisions and a tradition of *stare decisis* makes it difficult to determine in advance the type of sanctioned behaviour. In order to increase predictability, many bourses in the world federation have relaxed the norm of complete secrecy. Arbitrators publish written announcements of the principles used to decide novel cases while keeping the parties and other identifying facts secret'. Private dispute-resolution mechanisms are very flexible and diverse. They can even accommodate the demands for precedent setting while still meeting demands for privacy. However, privacy is not always as important as some critics of arbitration seem to believe.

Landes and Posner (1979), Brunet (1987) and others who see in ADR a failure to create external benefits appear to take the characteristics of some ADR and extrapolate them to all ADR, assuming that ADR is a much more homogeneous commodity than it really is. But if external benefits are significant there are strong incentives to internalize them, so when precedents become important institutional adjustments are likely to be made. Indeed, this provides one of the incentives to form groups such as trade associations and diamond bourses which clearly can internalize the benefits of precedents. Within such an organization, it is easy to imagine a contractual arrangement that creates incentives to minimize disputes by setting clear precedents (for example, consider arbitrators who compete to receive a lump-sum fee under a contract to handle all of the disputes between members of a particular organization over a particular period of time, or arbitrators chosen from the membership of an association who have

high opportunity costs if they encourage excessive disputes in the form of time spend away from their business pursuits, and who also personally benefit from clear precedents). When the environment is a dynamic changing one in which existing rules may frequently be inadequate guides for a new dispute, arbitration rulings are likely to be recorded and/or made known to the relevant group (which certainly is not likely to be the entire 'public', of course, but in general, that is not necessary or even desirable – the idea that a single universal system of law is somehow superior to polycentric law with parallel, as well as overlapping and competitive jurisdictions is not consistent with either theory or reality [Benson, 1990, 1992a, 1999b, 2000b; Berman, 1983]). This in turn creates incentives for ADR providers to make careful rulings based on recognized practices, customs and precedents established within the relevant group. For support of this hypothesis, consider international commercial arbitration. When no clear rule applies from 'the private international law systems from which the parties come' arbitrators must determine the appropriate new rule (Lew, 1978, p. 584). To do so, 'in their desire to make an award … acceptable and fair, arbitrators often try to show the inherent correctness of their decision in the award itself … arbitrators may refer to several rules to show how they all lead to the same result' (Lew, 1978, p. 584–585). Thus, international arbitration has characteristics often attributed to the common law, as arbiters look to past rulings, practices, traditions, and usage in extending the law to new issues – that is, in producing new precedent based on older law. In fact, the general view of international arbitrators is that, 'owing no allegiance to any sovereign State, international commercial arbitration has a special responsibility to develop and apply the law of international trade' (Lew, 1978, p. 589). But the same holds within many domestic trade associations. Indeed, the law-making consequences of private arbitration in the United States led Wooldridge (1970, p. 104) to suggest that its substantial growth in this century has involved a 'silent displacement of not only the judiciary but even the legislature'.

IV. Sanctions to Back ADR[5]

Another potential contradiction to the contentions that contracts and/or ADR can be a source of new substantive rules is the frequently made claim that in order to induce compliance with arbitration clauses in contracts and/or acceptance of arbitration rulings by the loser the other party must be willing and able to seek enforcement by some coercive power. For example, Landes and Posner (1979, p. 247) are among many who suggest that domestic arbitration in the United States must be backed by a threat to litigate. If litigation provides the relevant threat then the potential for creating new rules through contract and/or arbitration, and indeed, arbitration's potential as a jurisdictional choice, may be undermined even if judges never directly interpret most of the rules that are applied. After all, a credible threat to litigate requires that contractual clauses and arbitration rulings will be acceptable to judges, and therefore, they will have to correspond, at least to a degree, with expectations about how they will be viewed under judicial review. These claims are not correct, however, because 'non-legal sanctions' (Charny, 1990, p. 409–412) can induce the members of a 'community of transactors' to live up to contractual obligations and accept arbitration.

Repeated dealings create an environment conducive to the development of trust, for instance, and incentives to employ co-operative strategies. In addition, each individual enters into several different dealings with different trading partners, so refusal to live up to an obligation or to arbitrate within one transaction can affect the person's reputation and limit his ability to enter into other transactions. Essentially, anyone who chooses a non-cooperative strategy

---

[5] This section is drawn from Benson (1999b).

in one transaction will have difficulty finding a partner for any future transactions (Tullock, 1985, pp. 1075–1076). Therefore, in order to maintain a reputation for dealing under recognized rules of behaviour (that is, for fair and ethical dealings, including amicable acceptance of 'fair' non-violent dispute resolution), each transactor's dominant strategy is likely to be to co-operate in each transaction, whether it is a repeated or a one-shot deal.

Both commitments and reputation threats can also be made more credible, in many instances, if a group of individuals with mutual interests in long-term interaction form a 'contractual' organization such as a trade association. Such a group can provide a formal mechanism to overcome frictions in communication, insuring that information about any individual's non-cooperative behaviour will be transmitted to others in the relevant business community (Rubin, 1994, p. 24). Then group membership can include a contractual obligation to boycott anyone who fails to live up to a contractual obligation or reneges on a promise to arbitrate or accept an arbitration ruling: specifically, any noncooperative party will be *automatically* expelled from the organisation (Rubin, 1994, p. 24). Such automatic ostracism penalties make the reputation threat much more credible (Williamson, 1991, p. 168). These groups can also lower the transactions costs by establishing their own unbiased ADR arrangements (Bernstein, 1992; Benson, 1995, 1998a). For instance, arbitration selection mechanisms vary widely, but they all are designed to guarantee the selection of an unbiased arbitrator or arbitration tribunal that will apply the law that the contracting parties have explicitly or implicitly (by default) chosen.[6]

---

[6] Within some organizations, for instance, a single arbitrator or panel is chosen for a set period to arbitrate all disputes between members. Thus, pre-screening occurs as these arbitrators are chosen from a competitive pool by the association through its membership approved selection process (for example, see Bernstein, 1992, pp. 124–125). Those selected are likely to have considerable standing (reputation) within the community, and they have strong incentives to maintain

The roles of repeated dealing, reputation and of ostracism threats are obvious in many business communities, where they may even be formalized within trade associations or other organized groups. They are less obvious but still quite important in other 'communities' such as the neighbours of Shasta County, California (Ellickson, 1991). Viable private sanctions mean that customary law and ADR can escape the shadow of the law, but such sanctions vary considerably in strength. Circumstances that are likely to lead to effective private sanctions for some 'communities' and circumstances that may not in others are discussed at some length in Ellickson (1991) and Benson (1998a, 1999b), so a detailed discussion is not provided here. However, one determinant of the strength of private sanctions is worth noting. Time horizons are important determinants of the strength of potential reputation effects, as they are for discount rates in repeated-dealing

---

their own reputation for fairness, so they are not likely to be biased or corruptible. Another selection alternative involves a pre-approved list of professional arbitrators determined by the contracting parties or their trade organization, so if a dispute arises, an arbitrator is chosen from the list by some pre-set mechanism (for example, random selection, rotating selection, selection by a third party such as a governing board of the association). Empirical evidence indicates that selection of the pre-approved list is based on the reputation of the arbitrators for impartiality and expertise in contractual matters that might arise (Ashenfelter, 1987; Bloom and Cavanagh, 1986). Another common selection system gives the parties to a dispute the résumés of an odd numbered list of arbitrators from a larger pre-selected group (for instance, pre-selected by a trade association, or provided by an organization like the ICC or the AAA), with each party having the power to veto names successively until one remains. Thus, a second level of screening is added at the time of the dispute, contributing 'to the legitimacy of the arbitrator and his award in the eyes of the parties' (Bloom and Cavanagh, 1986, p. 409). Since the parties are given the arbitrator's résumés, they have information about experience, training, the nature of awards given in the past, and so on. Other selection procedures also exist, but all such systems are intended to guarantee the appointment of an arbitrator without requiring explicit agreement by the two parties while still allowing for pre-screening, and possible more than one level of screening, of potential arbitrators.

reciprocities. Therefore, incentives to invest in building a reputation are significantly weakened when the decision makers' time horizons are short, and high levels of uncertainty tend to undermine the potential for private sanctions such as threats to reputation or long-term reciprocities. Rubin (1994, p. 32) explains that much of this uncertainty reflects political instability. When property rights are unstable due to potential opportunistic behaviour by government (for example, changes in tax policy to capture the quasi-rents that arise with investments in reputation), or to such things as governments' inability or unwillingness to prevent counterfeiting and trademark infringements, incentives to invest in reputation are weak so threats of private sanctions are likely to be weak. A government can also raise the costs of using private sanctions. For instance, the use of boycotts or the distribution of certain types of information could be declared illegal. To the degree that rules against such private actions can be enforced, private sanctions may be insufficient inducements to accept ADR. Thus, if judges or legislators perceive ADR to be a threat to their power because it serves as a mechanism for implementing the law of an alternative jurisdiction, they can undermine its potential impact by attacking it directly – and there are many historical examples of such attacks (Benson, 1989, 1995, 1998c) or indirectly by weakening the ability to impose sanctions in the private communities that might use such alternatives. These attempts to undermine interjuris-dictional competition are undesirable, however, in contrast to the beliefs of many who contend that a single legal system within a geographic jurisdiction is superior to a polycentric system with many identifiable customary law communities.

V. Benefits of Interjurisdictional Competition through ADR[7]

A monocentric legal system is often seen as desirable. After all, rules can be 'harmonized' and 'unified' and duplication of services (such as, courts) can be reduced. There are at least three reasons for resistance to such monopolized law, however. First, the wide variety of activities and relationships that exist in a modern world mean that many rules that are effective for one type of transaction or one group may not be effective for another. Consider the diamond traders discussed by Bernstein (1992) and the oil traders discussed by Trakman (1983), for instance. The products being traded within these commercial communities are very different, suggesting that very different contractual issues are likely to be relevant, but the trading communities are also very different. Diamond merchants share common ethnic and religious backgrounds, creating an environment of mutual understanding (for example, of common trade practices and usage) and trust, for instance, thus reducing the need for highly technical and specific contracts, while oil traders display much greater ethnic and religious diversity as well as differences in motivations (a number of oil-producing states have nationalized production, for example, so political considerations can have major impacts on decision-making), possibly reducing the level of common understanding and undermining trust relationships, thus dictating much more specific and complex contracts. These two commercial groups are likely to share many of the same rules but there are also likely to be some important differences in traditions and practices. Indeed, imposition

---

[7] This section is drawn from Benson (2000c). For additional discussion and elaboration, see Benson (1999b, 2000a, 2000b, 2000d).

of the diamond merchants' contractual rules and governance institutions on the oil traders would probably lead to higher transactions costs for these traders, including more contract disputes, while imposition of the oil traders' rules on the diamond merchants probably would add unnecessary complexity and costs to their contracting process. Combining all of the rules from each group under a monopolized legal system would create unnecessary complexity for both communities of traders. Nationalized legal systems tend to produce homogenized although very complex law that limits the potential for specialization. But as Cooter (1994, p. 216) explains, more decentralized law-making is desirable in the increasingly complex world that we live in. In other words, one reason for avoiding monopolization of law is that economies of standardization are not nearly as significant as some contend (for example, Landes and Posner [1979]), and they are probably shrinking, while the benefits of specialization are relatively large and growing.

A second but closely related point is that a monopoly in law will have undesirable results in a dynamic uncertain world. For instance, given the potential for 'bad' rules (for example, biased or transactions-cost-increasing rules) to be produced and maintained no matter what size the legal system is, the effects of such laws are less severe in a decentralized or polycentric system of legal jurisdictions. As Osterfeld notes (1989, p. 152), in the case of a 'good' rule, it often does not matter how extensive the legal system is, as good rules tend to be emulated, especially if there is competition for members and freedom to choose among jurisdictions. In the case of a bad rule, however, the extent of the legal system clearly matters, particularly if there are institutional factors that make elimination of such rules difficult. Furthermore, in the absence of alternatives, it may not be possible to evaluate the 'goodness' or 'badness' of a rule. A rule imposed in an over-arching legal system may produce undesirable unintended consequences that another rule would not produce, but this may not be recognized. On the other hand, as individuals in parallel legal systems

experiment with alternatives, the relative impacts of different rules can be observed and more effectively evaluated. Judges in the common law system, with its numerous jurisdictions (for example, 49 of the 50 US states – Louisiana has a civil law system – plus the federal common law, along with the jurisdictions in Great Britain, Canada, Australia and other former British Colonies) have clearly looked to evolving rules in other jurisdictions, for example, and many rules have spread from jurisdiction to jurisdiction while others that are tried in some jurisdictions are rejected by others. Centralization of law, perhaps through legislation or a single hierarchical court system, eliminates the benefits that arise from such experimentation, and in this regard, customary law supported through ADR can be a very important source of the rules adopted by national legal systems. Indeed, much of the law that has been codified or recognized as precedent in national legal systems actually derives from custom (Berman, 1983; Benson, 1989, 1992b, 1998b, 1999a). Today, however, courts will not enforce obligations derived solely from contracts and custom (Chen, 1992, p. 100), choosing instead to apply politically-motivated statute or precedent law where a conflict with custom arises. Thus the choice of a customary law jurisdiction often requires the use of ADR.

This brings us to the third and probably most significant reason for avoiding monopolization of law. Coase (1960) emphasizes that one motivation for creating rules is to eliminate externalities and facilitate voluntary interaction, but he also explains that rules and institutions determine the distribution of bargaining power and therefore the distribution of wealth. While he did not focus on this issue, these distributional consequences also create incentives to make and alter rules, as emphasized in the rent-seeking literature that has evolved from Tullock's (1967) insights. In fact, the politicized 'law' of nation states almost always reflects the conflicting efforts to achieve both objectives (Benson, 1999a, 2000b).

Unlike voluntary joint production and exchange which tends to increase wealth, involuntary wealth transfers

through enforcement of legislated rules within a monopolized legal jurisdiction, whether the rules are established by kings, dictators, 'representative' parliaments, or courts, tend to reduce wealth for at least four reasons. *First*, transfers (for instance, through a tax and/or subsidy, through trade barriers and other limits on competition such as licences and exclusive franchises, and through other similar discriminatory 'legal' actions) produce deadweight losses. *Second*, while many observers suggest that these deadweight losses are small and that institutions should evolve to minimize them, Becker (1983) and Tullock (1967), for example, explain that the resources consumed in the competition for such transfers also have opportunity costs. Individuals and groups have incentives to invest time and resources in an effort to gain wealth through the political process, and victims of the transfer process have incentives to defend their property rights. Part of these defence costs are rent-avoidance costs arising through investments in political information and influence, but exit is another option. Exit can be achieved by moving to an alternative political jurisdiction, or by hiding economic activity and wealth (for example, moving transactions 'underground' into black markets). Therefore, in order to induce compliance with discriminatory transfer rules, the rule makers will generally have to rely on an enforcement bureaucracy, both to prevent exit (for instance, establish a monopoly in law) and to execute the rules. These enforcement costs are a *third* source of opportunity costs that accompany a wealth-transfer process. Rules that facilitate voluntary production and exchange (such as private property rights and enforceable contracts) also require some enforcement costs, of course, but the level of these costs increases dramatically when laws are also imposed in order to generate involuntary wealth transfers.

The *fourth* source of costs may be the most significant, however. Faced with the probability of involuntary transfers, productive individuals' property rights to their resources, wealth, and income flows are perceived to be relatively insecure, so their incentives to invest in maintenance of and

improvements to their assets, and their incentives to earn income and produce new wealth that might be appropriated, are relatively weak. If transfers are expected to be large, frequent, and arbitrary, most wealth production actually may have to be motivated by threats (as under slavery or totalitarian socialism), making enforcement costs even higher. Such threats are imperfect, however, so production will be low and wealth expansion will be slow compared to a situation wherein property rights are relatively secure.

Perhaps a monopoly in law will not necessarily produce biased rules for the purpose of transferring wealth, but a necessary prerequisite for such law is strong barriers to exit for those who expect to lose wealth through transfers. Interjurisdictional competition can occur between legal systems attempting to monopolize law-making and enforcement, and to the degree that wealth can escape one to move to another, the potential for using law as a transfer mechanism is limited. This is another obvious benefit of interjurisdictional competition, and importantly, there is another source of competition as well, as suggested above: customary law can be produced and supported by institutions which are not attempting to monopolize law, and these legal systems offer an alternative to escape the jurisdictions of those who seek such monopolies.[8]

---

[8] In law, as in markets, competition is an important determinant of the outcome. Indeed, the benefits of competition go beyond the enhanced abilities to evaluate and choose among rules. Competition actually stimulates legal innovation and sophistication, as Berman (1983, p. 10) explains:

> It is this plurality of jurisdictions and legal systems that makes the supremacy of law both necessary and possible. ...The very complexity of a common legal <u>order</u> containing diverse legal <u>systems</u> contributes to legal sophistication. Which court has jurisdiction? Which law is applicable? How are legal differences to be reconciled? Behind the technical questions lay important political and economic considerations. ...The pluralism of ... law, ... has been ... a source of development, or growth – legal growth as well as political and economic growth.

References

Ashenfelter, Orley (1987) 'Arbitration behaviour', *American Economic Review, Papers and Proceedings*, vol. 77, pp. 342–346.

Becker, Gary S. (1983) 'A Theory of competition among pressure groups for political influence', *Quarterly Journal of Economics*, vol. 98, pp. 371–400.

Benson, Bruce L. (1989) 'The spontaneous evolution of commercial law', *Southern Economic Journal*, vol. 55, pp. 644–661.

Benson, Bruce L. (1990) *The Enterprise of Law: Justice without the State*. San Francisco: Pacific Research Institute.

Benson, Bruce L. (1992a) 'Customary law as a social contract: international commercial law', *Constitutional Political Economy*, vol. 2, pp. 1–27.

Benson, Bruce L. (1992b) 'The development of criminal law and its enforcement: public interest or political transfers', *Journal des Economistes et des Etudes Humaines*, vol. 3, pp. 79–108.

Benson, Bruce L. (1995) 'An exploration of the impact of modern arbitration statutes on the development of arbitration in the United States', *Journal of Law, Economics, & Organisation*, vol. 11, pp. 479–501.

Benson, Bruce L. (1998a) 'Arbitration in the shadow of the law', in *The New Palgrave Dictionary of Economics and the Law*, edited by Peter Newman. London: Macmillan Press.

Benson, Bruce L. (1998b) 'Evolution of commercial law', in *The New Palgrave Dictionary of Economics and the Law*, edited by Peter Newman. London: Macmillan Press.

Benson, Bruce L. (1998c) 'Law merchant', in *The New Palgrave Dictionary of Economics and the Law*, edited by Peter Newman. London: Macmillan Press.

Benson, Bruce L. (1998d) *To Serve and Protect: Privatization and Community in Criminal Justice*. New York: New York University Press.

Benson, Bruce L. (1999a) 'An economic theory of the evolution of governance, and the emergence of the state', *Review of Austrian Economics*, vol. 12, pp. 131–160.

Benson, Bruce L. (1999b) 'To arbitrate or to litigate: That is the question', *European Journal of Law and Economics*, vol. 8, pp. 91–151.

Benson, Bruce L. (2000a) 'Arbitration', in *The Encyclopedia of Law and Economics*, edited by Boudewijn Bouckaert and Gerrit De Geest. London: Edward Elgar, forthcoming.

Benson, Bruce L. (2000b) 'Common law versus judge-made law', *Florida State University Working Paper*.

Benson, Bruce L. (2000c) 'Jurisdictional choice in international trade: implications for *Lex Cybernatoria*', *Journal des Economistes et des Etudes Humaines*, forthcoming.

Benson, Bruce L. (2000d) 'Polycentric law versus monopolised law: implications from international trade for the potential success of emerging markets', *Journal of Private Enterprise*, forthcoming.

Berman, Harold J. (1983) *Law and Revolution: The Formation of Western Legal Tradition*. Cambridge, MA: Harvard University Press.

Berman, Harold J. and Dasser, Felix J. (1990) 'The "new" law merchant and the "old": sources, content, and legitimacy', in *Lex Mercatoria and Arbitration: A Discussion of the New Law Merchant*, edited by Thomas E. Carbonneau. Dobbs Ferry, NY: Transnational Juris Publications.

Bernstein, Lisa (1992) 'Opting out of the legal system: extralegal contractual relations in the diamond industry', *Journal of Legal Studies*, vol. 21, pp. 115–158.

Bloom, David E. and Cavanagh, Christopher L. (1986) 'An analysis of the selection of arbitrators', *American Economic Review*, vol. 76, pp. 408–422.

Böckstiegal, K.H. (1984) *Arbitration and State Enterprises: A Survey of the National and International State of Law and Practice*. Deventer, Netherlands: Kluwer Law and Taxation Publishers.

Brunet, Edward (1987) 'Questioning the quality of alternative dispute resolution', *Tulane Law Review*, vol. 62, pp. 1–56.

Casella, Alessandra (1992) 'Arbitration in international trade', *Center for Economic Policy Research Discussion Paper*, no. 721, London.

Charny, David (1990) 'Nonlegal sanctions in commercial relationships', *Harvard Law Review*, vol. 104, pp. 373–467.

Chen, J. C. (1992) 'Code, custom, and contract: the uniform commercial code as law merchant', *Texas International Law Journal*, vol. 27, pp. 91–135.

Coase, Ronald H. (1960) 'The problem of social cost', *Journal of Law and Economics*, vol. 3, pp. 1–44.

Cooter, Robert D. (1994) 'Structural adjudication and the new law merchant: a model of decentralised law', *International Review of Law and Economics*, vol. 14, pp. 215–231.

David, R. (1985) *Arbitration in International Trade*. Deventer, The Netherlands: Kluwer Law and Taxation Publishers.

de Soto, Hernando (1989) *The Other Path: The Invisible Revolution in the Third World*. New York: Harper & Row.